THE USED CAR GUIDE

Also By Phil Edmonston

Lemon-Aid

THE USED CAR GUIDE

Best Buys, Lemons, Confidential Prices, Rusting Diagrams

Phil Edmonston

BEAUFORT BOOKS, INC.
New York • Toronto

Copyright © 1982 by Phil Edmonston
All rights reserved. No part of this publication may be reproduced or transmitted in any form or by any means, electronic or mechanical, including photocopy, recording, or any information storage and retrieval system now known or to be invented, without permission in writing from the publisher, except by a reviewer who wishes to quote brief passages in connection with a review written for inclusion in a magazine, newspaper, or broadcast.

Library of Congress Cataloging in Publication Data
Edmonston, Louis-Philippe.
The used car guide.

1. Used cars—Purchasing.   I. Title.
TL162.E333   629.2'222   81-4543
ISBN 0-8253-0051-7   AACR2

Published in the United States by Beaufort Books, Inc., New York.
Published simultaneously in Canada by General Publishing Co. Limited

Printed in the U.S.A.   First U.S. Edition
1 3 5 7 9 10 8 6 4 2

Designed by Joy Chu

CONTENTS

ACKNOWLEDGMENTS	v
INTRODUCTION	1
How to Use This Guide	5
Part 1: How to Choose the Right Used Car for You	**7-69**
Is a Car Really Necessary?	9
Will That Be Cash or Charge?	11
Why Buy a Used Car?	13
Choosing the Right Time	25
Choosing the Seller	26
Choosing the Car	36
Active vs. Passive Auto Safety	60
Manufacturer's Responsibility for Used Cars	68
Part 2: Used Car Ratings	**71-188**
Definitions of Terms Used in Ratings	73
The 1979 and 1980 Models	80
American Models	81-133
General Motors Subcompacts	81-85
Vega	82
Chevette	83
Ford Subcompacts	85-93
Pinto/Bobcat	85
Fiesta	90
Capri	92
Chrysler Subcompacts	94-97
Colt/Arrow	94
Omni/Horizon	96
American Motors Subcompacts	97-101
Gremlin/Spirit	98
Pacer	100
General Motors Compacts	101-107
Citation, Omega, Skylark, and Phoenix	101
Nova	103

Ventura	104
Camaro	106
Ford Compacts	108-113
Maverick/Comet	108
Granada/Monarch	109
Mustang	111
Fairmont/Zephyr	111
Chrysler Compacts	113-117
Valiant	113
Dart	114
Volaré/Aspen	115
American Motors Compacts	117-119
Hornet/Concord	117
General Motors Intermediates	119-122
Chevelle/Malibu	119
LeMans	120
Chrysler Intermediates	122-123
LeBaron/Diplomat	122
General Motors Large Cars	123-127
Impala/Caprice	123
Delta 88/Royale	125
LeSabre/Electra/Century	126
Ford Large Cars	127-128
Custom/Galaxie	127
Chrysler Large Cars	128-130
Fury	128
General Motors Luxury Cars	130-131
Monte Carlo/Grand Prix	130
Ford Luxury Cars	131-133
Thunderbird	131
Foreign Models	**133-191**
British	133-137
British Leyland	133-137
Austin Marina	134
MGB	134
Triumph	134
French	138-143
Peugeot	138
Peugeot 504	138

Renault	140
Renault 5	142
Renault 12	141
German	144-155
BMW	144
BMW 320i	144
Mercedes Benz	146
Mercedes Benz 220D and 240D	147
Volkswagen	148
Audi	148
Beetle/Rabbit	150
Porsche	154
Italian	155-162
Alfa Romeo	155
Sedan 2000	156
Fiat	157
Fiat 124/128	157
Sports Cars and Sedans	160
Japanese	162-180
Datsun	162
Datsun B210	163
Datsun "Z" Cars	163
Honda	165
Honda Civic	167
Honda Accord	167
Mazda	173
Mazda GLC	174
Subaru	176
Toyota	178
Corolla/Tercel	178
Celica	179
Swedish	180-188
Saab	180
Saab 99	181
Volvo	182
Volvo 242	187
Volvo 264	188
APPENDIX	189-191
Selling a Car Without Fear and Loathing	189
How to Write a Good Want Ad	190

Parts of this book would have been impossible to complete were it not for information from the files of the Automobile Protection Association, and confidential information sent to me by automobile industry "whistle blowers."

INTRODUCTION

Frankly, I don't like cars. They are overpriced, high-polluting, unsafe machines that enslave rather than liberate mankind. The omnipresent automobile industry does not impress me either. Too often have I heard auto-industry executives who praise the free enterprise system and castigate consumers as "the nut behind the wheel." These same executives are capable of performing amazing feats of Orwellian "double-think" by condemning government intervention in the industry as a "socialist plot" while continually asking the government for welfare in the form of tax exemptions, anti-competitive tariffs, and outright subsidies.

Ideally, we all would be better off without automobiles. But many of us need automobiles for our work, and the country is so vast that mass transit systems are woefully inadequate. So the purchase of an automobile is a necessity for many citizens who are mindful of the antisocial effects of the "infernal combustion engine," but have no other alternative.

Since the automobile industry is apparently a necessary evil, the best weapon the consumer can use to minimize his or her losses is court action. Businessmen, represented by the Better Business Bureau, deny this. They prattle about the uselessness of confrontation and how all the average intelligent consumer needs for protection is product information. As a result, you see groups such as the BBB "informing" consumers about used-car purchases with such generalities as "investigate before you invest," and similar banalities.

Granted, information is necessary for consumers wishing to make an intelligent choice when faced with competing products. When, however, did the auto industry voluntarily give out the hard facts about its cars and dealers that most consumers need in order to make a reasoned decision as to which new or used car should be purchased? One needs only to look at advertising on television and in print to see that the only information these media disseminate through car ads is sexist (new cars becoming an extension of our libidinal fantasies where beautiful women become pushovers if the right model car is purchased), misleading (sure

Ford's 1978 Pinto *may* get 30 miles to the gallon of gas under ideal conditions, if the kids and mother-in-law don't ride along), and irrelevant (what *is* General Motors' "Mark of Excellence"? Surely not their Citation or Chevette models. Ford's "Better Idea" is surely not premature rusting!).

Used-car buyers looking for factual information, therefore, cannot find much helpful information from the industry-dominated consumer protection agencies like the BBB or from the manufacturers themselves through their television and newspaper advertising. But what about car magazines and books? There are about 70 automobile magazines on the market. Most of these magazines are dominated by the automobile industry through advertising revenue that is solicited from the major car manufacturers. Advertising revenue represents about 75 percent of the entire annual revenue that some of these special interest publications require to stay in business. Private subscriptions may account for about 25 percent of the total annual revenue. So, for each consumer vote, there may be 3 votes coming from the auto industry.

Take car columnists, for example. Many major newspapers across North America offer their readers information of special appeal to automobile enthusiasts by employing an automobile columnist. Theoretically, this idea is a good one, and the stated purpose of informing the motoring public is to be encouraged.

However, in practice, many North American car columnists do nothing more than rewrite and publish the constant stream of biased and misleading press releases emanating from the automobile industry. Very little investigative reporting is carried out, because that type of public-interest journalism does not sell advertising, takes considerable effort, and will result in the drying up of information sources within the industry.

The "Car of the Year"

This rating has been used so often that it has started to get out of hand. Recently, *Motor Trend* decided to choose ten cars of the year as a special bonus to its subscribers. Even the automobile industry's trade paper, *Automotive News*, had to step in with an editorial blasting the whole concept of choosing a car of the year. In essence, the criticism of the practice centered on the fact that different drivers have different needs and appreciate cars on a purely subjective basis. Therefore, every car ever produced could be the car of the year for somebody.

Once again *Motor Trend* magazine has used its car of the year award that is so well appreciated by its advertising manager and the auto industry alike. In fact, judging from M.T.'s previous car of the year awards, one can almost expect the "car of the year" to be more of a "lemon of the year." Let's take 1978 for example. *Motor Trend* designated the 1978 Omni/Horizon as "car of the year," unfortunately this award was made before the car was delivered to the public according to the June 1978 edition of *Automotive News*.

Consumers Union, also stupefied by M.T.'s award to Chrysler, had the following scathing comment for *Motor Trend*'s "car of the year."

> Most years, the commercial backscratching that sometimes passes for journalism, or even for product testing can be ignored; it's just a drop in the ocean of flackery. But sometimes, as this year, those who take such flackery seriously risk paying with more than their dollars.

Still, what do you expect from the magazine that gave the "car of the year" award to General Motors' ill-fated Vega.

Donald MacDonald, former editor of *Motor Trend* magazine describes the "dubious charade" of the Car of the Year magazine awards in the following terms: "... Car of the Year magazine awards as well as Import Car of the Year, Truck of the Year, ad nauseum, from all the magazines that jumped into the act, went to the highest bidder. To be sure, winners can generally be justified on technical grounds, but so too can some of the losers. It became a matter of which manufacturer would plug the magazine and its award the hardest on TV and billboards and, most importantly, which would commit to the biggest advertising schedule in the donor's magazine. Only *Road & Track*, bless its stuffy integrity, stayed consistently aloof..." (Donald MacDonald, *Detroit 1985*, Doubleday & Company, New York, N.Y., 1980).

Automobile testing done by most popular car magazines is carried out over a period of a week or two. The car is supplied by the manufacturer and tuned to just the right specifications. Of course, the dealer's servicing of the vehicle will be impeccable. Finally, the manufacturer will probably load the car with an assortment of expensive options to compensate for any of the vehicle's obvious faults.

With this rigged test, the car maker cannot lose. And if the tester wants other free courtesy cars to test, the published report had better gloss over the more obvious vehicle defects and treat in the superlative some of the car's more mediocre features. Also, if the magazine or newspaper receives advertising from the manufacturer, any criticism that gets through the driver's own self-censorship will be muted by the editor. Another very important reason for discounting these tests is that they cannot predict a car's vulnerability to rust, poor servicing, or inadequate parts distribution.

Although these publications will say this criticism of their operations is unfair, one merely has to read their back issues to realize that these magazines suffer from a serious conflict of interest when they evaluate new cars and publish automobile industry press releases. Does this conflict of interest mean that a car magazine is not honest with its readers? No, not exactly. What it means is that the magazine may have to write its criticism with one ear cocked to the side waiting for the vote of confidence or outrage that is sure to come from the auto industry in reaction to its articles. Consequently, many publications seem to practice the art of self-censorship to such a degree that a car's mediocre performance may be called "unique" and a real "lemon" such as the 1975 Rabbit/Scirocco from Volkswagen may only be criticized after the most horrendous breakdowns occur.

Automotive books are helpful, though, if their information is current and taken from unbiased sources. This means that reliable car guides must be published annually and get their funding and information primarily from consumers. Even Consumers Union, which publishes an excellent April *Buying Guide*, frequently designates cars as good buys when, in fact, these same cars have been real lemons. The competency of a particular company's dealership body cannot be effectively evaluated by one consumer group alone.

One place where consumers are likely to find solid facts relating to the purchase of a new or used car is the Automobile Protection Association, a nonprofit, public-interest corporation, based in Montreal. The group receives from 75,000 to 100,000 auto complaints and inquiries yearly. These complaints are tabulated according to models, years, and dealerships that are implicated. Much of the APA's material is used in an annual automotive guide called *Lemon-Aid*.

Because of all the possible ways one can be cheated in buying and operating a new car, I advise consumers to purchase good used cars, instead. At least, with a used car there is a greater chance of learning about the quality of the product, the initial investment is less than for a new car, and you can always sue the seller in small-claims court or county court where costs are low and waiting periods relatively short.

Much of the information concerning used-car defects has been culled from the files of the Automobile Protection Association and the Washington-based Center for Auto Safety. Other information relating to product liability and warranty disputes has been taken from court judgments, consumer group research projects, government studies, and complaints sent to Consumers Union by readers of *Consumer Reports.*

After personally interviewing thousands of consumers and participating in trials as an expert witness throughout North America, I remain firmly convinced that buying a good used car is the only way to beat the auto industry at its own game. I am so sure of this that two years ago, I bought two used cars: a 1977 Buick LeSabre ($3000) and a 1975 Dodge Dart ($2000). I have never regretted this $5000 investment.

How to Use This Guide

This used-car guide will help to protect you from buying a defective car or paying too much, if you take the following steps:

1. Decide which car meets your needs and budget. When figuring how much money should be budgeted, try not to exceed 15 percent of your gross annual income. Only cash should be considered.

2. Check local want ads, bulletin board announcements, and make discreet inquiries among friends and neighbors. A used-car dealer is the last person to see.

3. Verify the selling price. These confidential selling prices are listed according to model and year. Don't stray more than 10 percent away from the price listed in this book, no matter how good the car looks.

4. Order an independent mechanical inspection. This must be done *before* the car is purchased. Give particular attention to the performance-related defects noted in this guide.

5. Make a thorough rust inspection. Use the services of either a mechanic or specialized body repairman. Do not examine the car yourself. Rust damage is easily hidden and cannot always be detected by the untrained eye. This inspection must also be done *prior* to purchasing the vehicle.

6. Check for recalls. More than 80 million cars have been recalled for safety-related defects. The manufacturer is obligated to repair for free any used car if it was one of the estimated 25 million vehicles that the

Ministry of Transportation believes has never been repaired. Write the Ministry of Transportation and Communications, Motor Vehicle and Traffic Safety Branch, Ottawa, Ontario.

7. Check for warranty extensions. When automobile manufacturers extend their car warranty to cover the premature breakdown of specific vehicle components, they often include owners who may have bought their car used. General Motors' 200-series transmission warranty extension and Ford's engine warranty extension both apply to used vehicles.

8. Note the gas mileage. This guide lists the approximate gas mileage reported by consumers driving similar models. This mileage can vary from 15 to 20 percent as a result of poor dealer servicing, the condition of the vehicle, and outside temperatures. If actual gas mileage is far inferior to the mileage indicated in this guide, check for a defective mechanical component. If the vehicle is defective by design, it is possible to go to the small-claims court where damages can be claimed for the extra gas that was used.

PART ONE

How to Choose the Right Used Car for You

IS A CAR REALLY NECESSARY?

Before purchasing a used car you should make sure that you really need an automobile. Few people realize that automobile ownership may be so frustrating that it can make driving a nightmare.

The following information, supplied by the American Automobile Association, gives some statistics on the national average costs involved in owning and operating a car:

Automobile Operating Costs

Here is a breakdown by national average costs computed in February 1980 by Runzheimer and Co. (a Rochester, Wisconsin, management-consulting firm), for a 1980 Chevrolet, 6-cylinder (229 cu. in.) Malibu Classic 4-door sedan with standard accessories, automatic transmission, power steering, power disc brakes, and radio, driven up to 15,000 miles per year. Gasoline costs are based on $1.22 per gallon. Insurance is based on a pleasure use category where the vehicle is driven less than 10 miles to or from work and there is no youthful operator.

Variable Costs	*Average per mile*
Gasoline (unleaded) and oil	5.86 cents
Maintenance	1.12 cents
Tires	.64 cents
	7.62 cents

Fixed Costs	*Annually*
Comprehensive insurance ($100 ded.)	$ 70.00
$250 ded. collision insurance	172.00
Property damage and liability ($100/300/50M)	248.00
License, registration, taxes	82.00
Depreciation	1038.00
Finance charge (20% down; loan @ 15%/4 yrs.)	423.00
	$2033.00
	(or $5.57 per day)

While some fixed costs are the same even if the car remains parked in the garage, the more you drive the less the per-mile cost will be. Conversely, a reduction in mileage will raise the per-mile cost.

Add-ons.
Air conditioning: 15 cents per mile and 20 cents per day.
Depreciation for excess mileage: $43 per thousand miles over 15,000 annually. (The $1038 is an average based on trade-in at the end of four years or 60,000 miles, whichever comes first. This is the period during which the car is expected to deliver the greatest economy.)

Average Annual Driving Costs.
Based on the figures above, the motorist driving 15,000 miles a year would pay:

```
15,000 miles @ 7.62 cents .............................. $1143.00
365 days @ $5.57 ......................................  2033.00
                                                         $3176.00
                                            (or 21.2 cents per mile)
```

The same person driving 10,000 miles a year would pay:

```
10,000 miles @ 7.62 cents .............................. $ 762.00
365 days @ $5.57 ......................................  2033.00
                                                         $2795.00
                                              (or 28 cents per mile)
```

In addition to the constant worry of possibly being killed by a car that loses its wheels, explodes, catches fire, or suddenly careens out of control, there is always the possibility that the car may inadvertently kill or injure someone else. Statistics from the Insurance Institute for Highway Safety actually predict that the average car is involved in at least two accidents before being taken off the road.

Automobile ownership means increased responsibilities. Insurance papers need to be filled out, government taxes paid, parking tickets stamped, periodic maintenance performed, accident reports filed, insurance claims settled, on-the-road breakdowns repaired, transportation expenses deducted, safety inspections done, new license plates purchased and old traffic tickets paid.

Car enthusiasts may point out that the responsibilities of car ownership are rewarded by the increased freedom of mobility that ownership gives. In some cases this may be true; however, it is difficult to believe that motorists stuck for hours in congested bumper-to-bumper traffic would agree that their cars represent individual freedom.

Another often overlooked effect of car ownership is its tendency to foster antisocial attitudes. When a car is purchased, it automatically becomes an extension of its owner and provides an artificial environment complete with life-support systems such as music, automatic climate control, automatic cruise control, electric windows that shut out extraneous air and noise, and speed with which to blur the passing scene. The average motorist is thus transformed into a self-sufficient entity, encapsulated in 3000 pounds of plastic and steel.

Once all the advantages and disadvantages of car ownership have been weighed and a decision to purchase has been made, proceed to the next step of deciding how much is to be spent and whether the purchase should be financed.

WILL THAT BE CASH OR CHARGE?

Anyone earning $10,000 or less should not spend more than $1500, or 15 percent of his/her annual income in purchasing a used car. The same logic applies to an individual earning $20,000 yearly. A good used car should not cost that individual more than $3000. Anybody spending more than 15 percent of his/her annual income (businessmen seeking tax advantages exempted), is throwing money out the window.

By keeping the initial cost of a used car between $1000 and $3000, the purchaser will be able to pay in cash and this cash will provide a key bargaining tool to use with private individuals selling their cars directly. However, used-car dealers are not as impressed by cash bargaining because they get a kickback from the finance companies based upon the volume and amount of finance business they write up. A portion of the life insurance premium that is used to protect some financed deals may also be given back to the dealer as part of the sales commission.

Sometimes it is not possible to buy a car with cash. If this is the situation, it would be well to study the advantages and disadvantages of the following lending institutions:

Credit Unions. This is probably the preferred place to borrow money at low interest rates and with easy repayment terms. One of the major difficulties with some credit unions is that they may require that you be a member of the union or have an account with them before lending you any money. An application may also be refused if the credit union discovers you are a poor credit risk.

TABLE 1
What It Will Cost You to Finance Your Car

$	12 Months	18 Months	24 Months	30 Months
1000	103.02/ 91.92	152.80/ 64.04	203.98/ 50.19	256.57/ 41.89
1500	154.53/137.88	229.20/ 96.07	305.98/ 75.25	384.85/ 62.83
2000	206.03/183.84	305.60/128.09	407.97/100.33	513.13/ 83.77
2500	257.54/229.80	382.00/160.11	509.96/125.42	641.42/104.71
3000	309.05/275.75	458.40/192.13	611.95/150.50	769.70/125.66
3500	360.56/321.71	534.80/224.16	713.95/175.58	897.98/146.60
4000	412.07/367.67	611.20/256.18	815.94/200.66	1026.27/167.54
4500	463.58/413.63	687.59/288.20	917.93/225.75	1154.55/188.48
5000	515.09/459.59	763.99/320.22	1019.92/250.83	1282.83/209.43
6000	618.10/551.51	916.79/384.27	1223.91/301.00	1539.40/251.31
7500	772.63/689.39	1145.99/480.33	1529.88/376.25	1924.25/314.14

$	36 Months	42 Months	48 Months	60 Months
1000	310.53/ 36.40	365.87/ 32.52	422.57/ 29.64	539.97/ 25.67
1500	465.80/ 54.61	548.81/ 48.78	633.86/ 44.46	809.96/ 38.50
2000	621.07/ 72.81	731.75/ 65.04	845.14/ 59.27	1079.95/ 51.33
2500	776.33/ 91.01	914.68/ 81.30	1056.43/ 74.09	1349.93/ 64.17
3000	931.60/109.21	1097.62/ 97.56	1267.72/ 88.91	1619.92/ 77.00
3500	1086.87/127.41	1280.57/113.82	1479.00/103.73	1889.90/ 89.83
4000	1242.13/145.61	1463.50/130.08	1690.29/118.55	2159.89/102.66
4500	1397.40/163.82	1646.43/146.34	1901.57/133.37	2429.88/115.50
5000	1552.67/182.02	1829.37/162.60	2112.86/148.18	2699.86/128.33
6000	1863.20/218.42	2195.24/195.12	2535.43/177.82	3239.84/154.00
7500	2329.00/273.03	2744.05/243.91	3169.29/222.28	4049.79/192.50

Cost of Borrowing shown in **Boldface** Figures
Monthly Payment Shown in Lightface
Interest Calculated at 18 percent per annum

Banks. Banks enjoy lending small loans to consumers who have average incomes and appear to be capable of paying off the loan. However, interest rates are comparably high, with repayment plans flexible. Bank loans are seldom made for more than 36 to 48 months. Banks are, however, sometimes willing to take chances with consumers who have never borrowed before or who have low incomes.

During the past year, the cost of credit charged by most banks for small, short-term loans has hovered around 18 to 20 percent. In calculating a bank loan's cost, use Table 1, which indicates interest costs and monthly payments.

Finance Companies. Many people are critical of finance companies because they charge excessive interest rates and seem to attract primarily low-income people as their customers. Although a finance company should be the *last* place one goes for a small, short-term loan, the fact remains that finance companies fill a consumer need that has been created by the restrictive lending policies of other lending institutions. The advantages of relaxed credit restrictions and quick loans appeal to many people who cannot get financing elsewhere.

WHY BUY A USED CAR?

The New-Car Jungle

Most consumers buy new cars mainly because they don't want to be stuck with "somebody else's troubles," or simply because they enjoy the status of owning a new automobile. Unfortunately, for many new-car purchasers, the status of owning a new car fades away just about when the neighbors buy their new car and the new car warranty protection promised by the manufacturer has turned into a flip-the-coin contest. So, the new-car purchaser may ultimately find out that in buying a new car he or she has still gotten stuck "with somebody else's troubles": the auto manufacturer's!

Why New-Car Warranties Don't Work

New-car warranties are made to sell cars, not to service them. One can clearly see this fact when examining the American automobile manufacturers' reaction to their realization that the 5-year/50,000-mile warranty was costing too much in the early '70s. It became evident at that time that cars covered by the warranty were not being built to last five years. So the automobile industry responded, not by improving the quality of their cars, but by dropping the five-year warranty.

The general decline in new-car quality is acting as a contributing factor in consumer discontent with warranties, but there are also other fundamental reasons that make new-car warranties practically worthless. For example:

The manufacturer is in a conflict-of-interest situation. Read most new-car warranties carefully and you will find such phrases as "Warranty does not cover owner misuse," "Does not cover lack of proper maintenance," "Does not cover consequential damages," and finally, "The warranty of the manufacturer is the only expressed warranty covering this vehicle." By sticking these key legal phrases into car warranties, automobile manufacturers are able to accept or reject warranty claims for almost any reason.

By refusing to be held responsible for consequential damages, the manufacturers try to limit their legal liability for damages caused by any defective components in their cars. Theoretically then, if the car has to be towed several hundred miles, or if serious injuries are caused in an accident, the new-car manufacturers will only replace or repair the defective part and leave the payment of consequential damages to the victim.

Automobile manufacturers insist that the law treat their own warranty as the only binding guarantee of quality and safety in their vehicles to reinforce their arbitrary power over customers contesting warranty decisions. Fortunately, the North American courts have held that in addition to the manufacturers' *expressed* warranty, a much stronger judicial *implied* warranty exists to protect customers from cars that accelerate when they should stop and stop when they should accelerate. The problem, though, with the common law implied warranty is that consumers must go through court to make sure that this warranty is applied. It is not surprising to see that most lawsuits are abandoned because consumers do not wish to take chances with courts that could prove to be expensive, time-consuming, and psychologically stressful. Apart from some isolated small-claims court victories, the new-car purchaser is ultimately stuck with the manufacturer's warranty.

Warranty repairs receive less compensation. The National Automobile Dealers' Association has complained that auto manufacturers pay dealers less for warranty repairs than it costs dealers to perform them. Because they do not wish to go broke repairing new cars at the lesser rate, some dealers place a low priority on the warranty repairs and concentrate upon retail repair customers first, leaving new cars out of service for weeks. Others may simply charge the customer the full retail rate for the repair and not make a warranty claim to the manufacturer.

Warranty repairs are done on a quota basis. Each dealership and regional zone has a monthly quota of allowable warranty repairs and this quota is directly related to the number of new units sold in that particular region within a particular period of time. This quota program is strictly followed by dealers who wish to stay in the good graces of the manufacturer. Auto manufacturers actually rate dealers "A," "B," or "C," according to the number and type of warranty claims that are sent in. If a dealer is ranked in the "C" category, most of his warranty claims are carefully checked by the head office and sometimes the defective part must be sent to the manufacturer's headquarters for approval of the claim. On the other hand, the "A"-rated dealers have their warranty claims routinely processed by the company without any demands for subsequent confirmation.

Many dealership-service managers don't know what to do with an out-of-the-ordinary repair problem. Consequently, the dealer may come up with all kinds of excuses in an attempt to convince the customer that the car is really behaving normally. These "reasonable explanations" for unreasonable car problems can require quite a stretch of the imagination. Take, for example, the testimony of one VW Rabbit owner, who was driving at normal highway speeds when

> ...my Rabbit suddenly "ran away" for about 10 to 15 seconds. Even though my accelerator pedal functioned normally, I had no control over the vehicle during these 15 seconds. Afterward, so much black smoke came from the exhaust that passing motorists blew their horns, flashed their lights, and held their noses to get my attention.
>
> I returned to the dealer who then changed my air filter that was saturated with oil. A week later, the VW mechanic who tested the car with me hinted that my problem was likely "behind the wheel."

Obviously, this customer was denied any warranty compensation.

Warranty not fully explained before purchase. With the possible exception of American Motors, all new-car warranties are written in legal jargon that would baffle many lawyers. Not only is the warranty itself incomprehensible to most people, but many automobile dealers will not give out the warranty information until the vehicle has been purchased.

Warranty inadequate for declining product quality. It's true, they aren't making cars like they used to. One merely has to take a stroll through any parking lot to discover 1975- to 1979-model General Motors cars with paint defects that give them a chicken-pox look, Ford models with so many rust holes they have free air conditioning, and Datsun B-210, 510, 240, and 260-Z models with rusty, biodegradable bodies.

Although the above-mentioned new car manufacturers have admitted in court that their vehicles were defective, they have each raised the defense that their responsibility ended when the regular 1-year/12,000 mile warranty period elapsed. Therefore, it is only logical that new cars in the future should not be expected to last longer than the period of guarantee given out by the manufacturer. It is a sobering thought that cars that would last barely 5 years in the early '70s may only last half that time in the early '80s.

In conclusion, it is evident that a new car is not a sound investment for most motorists because of the inadequate warranty coverage, declining quality control standards, and an almost total lack of information concerning the vehicle and its warranty at the pre-purchase stage. But would a used-car purchase be any different? Wouldn't the buyer of a used car fall prey to the same deceptive practices and lack of information? Let's look at some of the advantages and disadvantages of buying a used car.

Fifteen Good Reasons for Buying a Used Car

Obviously, selling and buying used cars is a profitable business. When practiced on a wholesale and retail level by professionals, this business has been known to create millionaires practically overnight. Nevertheless, anyone venturing into the used-car market without some professional guidance or knowledge is destined to be eaten alive by the fast-buck artists who thrive in the used-car industry.

Smart consumers who consider all the angles, examine the true wholesale and retail prices of automobiles, and insist upon a mechanical verification are never caught by the used-car sharks.

Some of the advantages in buying a used car, particularly from a private party, are:

1. Depreciation savings. If someone were to ask you to invest in stocks or bonds that were guaranteed to be worth less than half their initial purchase value after 2 years, you would probably tell him to get lost. But this is exactly the trap you are falling into when buying a new car that normally depreciates 30 percent the first year and 20 percent the second. Ask any insurance company claims manager and you will discover that with the exception of some cars (sports car, imports and high-performance models), most new cars are worth only half their original retail sales value after two years' use.

Perhaps the following illustration will help to show how new cars become infinitely more expensive than a good used car:

```
New Car Purchase Price ................ $10,000
Tax ..................................     800 (8 percent)
Total Price .......................... $10,800
```

Now, the motorist buying a new car is certain that the new-car warranty and status of owning a new car far outweighs any inconvenience that may be suffered through the ownership of a new car. He happily forks over the required $10,800 and takes possession of his new automobile.

For the used-car buyer, the situation is altogether different. That same vehicle can be purchased two years later as a used car, without the manufacturer's warranty, for almost half its original cost. Perhaps the following illustration will help show what happens:

```
Used Car Purchase Price
   (After 2 Years and 30,000 miles of use) .............. $5000
Tax ............................................... $ 400
Total Price ....................................... $5400
```

It is easy to see that the used-car buyer will get his car at half the price that the new-car purchaser paid. This is Detroit's little game of "Depreciation Dominoes" which makes thousands of new-car owners losers when their cars are scrapped in automobile accidents, while at the same time providing used-car buyers with two-year-old cars at half their original price with more than three-fourths of their original mileage left to run.

Generally, a new car is expected to run at least 125,000 to 150,000 miles in its lifetime. In order to force car owners to change cars as frequently as possible, the automobile manufacturers maximize the depreciation of new cars during the first three years of ownership. Therefore, whoever manages to sell his or her car within the first year or two of ownership is expected to recoup the losses with the low prices offered for the new models. Thus, we find consumers "buying up" every few years in order to purchase the latest-model car even though the new model may offer no advantages nor have any real differences (except for a $500–$700 increase on its price tag) than the model previously traded in.

Apart from price differences, older cars also have their own "mystique" which gives them a following no matter when they are sold. Many used-car buyers have become aware of the fact that car manufacturers are not building cars like they used to, and these motorists are anxious to drive and own certain cars that may be only ten years old but which seem destined to become classics in their own time. So, by choosing the right type of car, the smart car shopper will not only get an excellent used car at less than half its original cost, but may also realize a profit on the deal because that car could become a used-car classic. Some used cars that have become classics within a short period of time are:

> General Motors Camaro/Firebird, Monte Carlo
> Chrysler Valiant/Dart
> American Motors Matador and Javelin
> Ford Mustang, Thunderbird, and Edsel
> Datsun 2000 Sports Coupe and 510 Sedan
> Toyota Celica 2000
> Renault 12
> Volkswagen Beetle
> Mercedes-Benz Diesel
> Volvo 122
> Citroën

This list of recently produced cars that are considered to be used-car classics is by no means complete.

On the other hand, some used cars are "lemons" and have depreciated much more than the standard rate during the last three to four years. Some of these industry "jewels" have distinguished themselves by being badly styled, like the VW 4-11; others have also managed to inflict other miseries upon their owners, like unavailable parts, parts that cost their weight in silver, defective components, and dealerships just one step away from Vincent Price's Chamber of Horrors.

Some recent models that have become almost worthless are:

General Motors Vega
Chrysler Volaré/Aspen
American Motors Rambler and Pacer
Renault 16 and Renault 10
Fiat 128
Volkswagen 411, 412
British Leyland Marina
Mazda early rotary models

Fortunately, the average consumer will be able to steer clear of these industry "orphans" by checking the value of the car in the industry "Red Book," by insisting upon a complete mechanical inspection of the vehicle before it is purchased, and by demanding a fair guarantee just in case the car still has some surprises to offer.

2. The right to a mechanical examination. With both used and new cars, what you see is what you get. For most new-car buyers, the only thing that is seen is the dealer's new-car contract. Few dealers, if any, allow their customers to verify the mechanical and body condition of the new cars they deliver. This policy has been adopted by most new-car dealers because they know that many customers would refuse to accept many new cars that are manufactured because of the large number of quality control defects that are generally present. Consumers Union warns us to expect at least twenty defects with every new car purchase.

But with used cars, the situation is reversed. Not only does the average buyer get to see what he is purchasing, but, in most cases, a private party or dealer will feel obligated to allow the examination of the merchandise that is to be considered. This examination before purchase is a tremendous protection to the purchaser of an automobile because it allows the customer to evaluate, with the help of an independent mechanic, the cost of maintenance repairs; it will help the purchaser bargain down the price of the vehicle in relation to the cost of estimated repairs; and it will enable the used-car purchaser to budget realistically for repairs that have been diagnosed before the sale.

Certainly, the mechanical examination of a used vehicle prior to purchase may cost $25–$50; however, the investment is a wise one, especially if the used car is expected to cost several thousand dollars. Remember, if the private owner or salesman does not want the car to be examined by an independent expert, run, don't walk, away. The seller is obviously trying to put something over on you. Don't fall for the standard excuses that the car is not insured, the license plates have expired, or the vehicle has a dead battery.

Remember, with a used car you have a right to inspect what you are buying. With a new car, you may have to make do with the dealer's new-car brochure instead.

3. Better parts availability and cheaper parts cost. When new cars are marketed in late September, the American manufacturers have not solved the logistics of supplying new parts for those cars for at least another six months. With some European and Japanese automakers, this delay may stretch even longer. This strange situation exists because new-car manufacturers concentrate most of their production on the manufacturing and marketing of their new models and turn their great production capacity to the manufacturing of replacement parts later in the model year. Of course, some production of replacement parts is carried out early in the model year run; however, it has been generally acknowledged that the automobile industry's primary target at this time is the new-car market, and replacement parts are secondary because those persons who may be clamoring for replacement parts are already stuck with their car and are no longer part of the new-car market.

Once again, the purchaser of a used car is faced with a different situation. After the first two or three years that a model has been sold, the replacement-parts market starts to overflow. This may occur because there are a number of cars involved in accidents where they are scrapped by the insurance company; or because of the number of similar used cars put up for sale on the used-car market. No matter the cause, after a few years, replacement parts are unquestionably easier to come by through bargaining with local dealers or through a careful search of junkyards (a used part bought from a junkyard may cost only one-third the price of that part new, and may also carry a guarantee).

4. Premature rusting can be detected. Many new cars fall prey to severe rusting long before they give out mechanically. But no new-car buyer can tell whether his new car is going to have rust problems or not.

This pitfall can be easily avoided when buying a used car. It only takes a careful examination by a trained car-body specialist to determine if the car has any serious rusting problems. Although this inspection may take only ten minutes, it can save hundreds of dollars in needless body repairs.

5. Better guarantees privately obtained. If the car is being bought from a private seller, it is unlikely that this individual has had much experience in cheating consumers through the selling of used cars. Thus, it is much easier to come away from the sale with a solid guarantee than if one were to do business with a professional car dealer. This is not to suggest that car dealers are thieves; however, it must be admitted that they have a lot more experience in defending their businesses before the courts for selling cars that were something less than "normal."

Consumers selling their cars through the want ads or elsewhere are generally law-abiding and may be very reluctant to doctor up a car's motor or transmission for a quick sale. Probably the most serious deception that can occur with private sales is tampering with the odometer to boost the selling price of the car. This type of everyday consumer fraud is like comparing shoplifting to the armed robbery that occurs everyday with professional used-car dealers who may be versed in a thousand and one ways of cheating the uninformed buyer.

Even if the used-car buyer falls victim to a deceptive representation made by a private owner, the law can protect that consumer from his own ignorance. However, if this same fraud has been perpetrated by a professional used-car con man, it is not likely that the law will be able to interfere with the terms and conditions of your contract unless it can be proven that the whole deal was made in bad faith with the intent to defraud. So, by benefiting from the protection of the law, used-car sharks may actually continue cheating their customers as long as it can be proved that there is no intent to defraud.

If the used-car dealer or private owner should attempt to misrepresent the quality of the used car, there are a number of state and federal laws that can be used to obtain a refund of the purchase price.

Incidentally, even if the used car is sold by a private owner and there is no deception involved, it is still possible that the vehicle may contain certain safety or performance-related defects that could render the original manufacturer of the vehicle responsible for any damages that may occur. For example, should the vehicle explode or careen out of control and this occurrence has been established as caused by the faulty manufacturing of the vehicle, the original manufacturer of the car can be held responsible.

6. Less initial cash outlay. In buying a car, one is simply buying transportation. The amount of the initial cash outlay is very important because it may take some of your spending income away from other areas where that income may obtain greater interest and be more productive. Because the purchase of many used cars only requires half the amount of cash or credit obligations that a new-car purchase requires, it is easy to see that the used-car purchaser need not invest as much income in a depreciating investment and may be fortunate enough to forgo entirely the need to take out a loan to finance the payments on a car. Both new- and used-car dealers receive considerable amounts of money from lending institutions and life insurance companies as commission based upon the amount of business they provide. For this fact alone, it is best to buy a used car that requires no more than a $2000 cash payment.

7. The seller may be inexperienced. People who sell their cars privately through newspaper want ads are not likely to know the real value of their cars nor have the experience with which to give you a misleading impression of the vehicle that is offered for sale. Usually the private owner just wants to get rid of the car as soon as possible in order to have the cash to use in some other business transaction.

When dealing with an inexperienced seller, one can always bargain down the price of the car for some of the most unlikely reasons. The best time for this tactic to be employed is during the inspection by an independent mechanic. Even if the automobile has been kept in the best of condition by an owner who followed all the periodic servicing instructions of the manufacturer, the independent mechanic will still find some mechanical deficiencies. And this discovery will no doubt unnerve the seller. Such routine maintenance items as new ball joints, brake linings, or a transmission overhaul in some high-mileage cars could make the car look like a potential "lemon" to its owner and will go a long way in sapping that owner's confidence in the car. This weakening of the confidence should be closely followed by a weakening of the seller's resistance to bargaining and could lower the price of the car by as much as $300 to $500.

Experienced used-car salesmen are immune to this trick because they practice it themselves when buying used cars off the street or when accepting used cars as a trade-in for a new car. An experienced used-car salesman would probably not allow the vehicle to be examined by an independent garage mechanic. However, if the car is examined and shows some minor mechanical deficiencies that salesman is likely to shrug off the criticism with the devastating reply: "So what do you expect with a *used* car?" And while you are feeling like a real pennypincher, that same salesman will probably start selling you on the idea that the vehicle is priced way below its wholesale price just because it has a few minor routine mechanical problems.

8. Cheaper insurance rates. Insurance companies know that collision repairs to a new car can be very expensive. Not only will it take weeks for some of the parts to arrive, but those parts will have to be bought new from the manufacturer who holds a monopoly on pricing and distribution of crash parts. As the recent hearings before the United States Senate have disclosed, new-car replacement parts prices have skyrocketed without any justifiable explanation on the part of the automobile manufacturers. Some insurance companies such as State Farm have accused the automakers of intentionally fixing prices through monopoly pricing and distribution practices.

The difference in cost for insurance between a new and used car may not seem much at first, but by carefully negotiating the deductibility claims the smart shopper can reduce insurance premiums by as much as $100 a year. For example, everyone knows that as a car gets older, the amount of deduction that the insured owner agrees to pay should be increased. This deduction may reach a maximum of $250 per collision. As the amount of deduction is increased, the annual premiums for collision coverage become cheaper.

By agreeing to the $250 deductible, the insured motorist agrees to repair the vehicle for all damages whose costs do not exceed the deductible. Generally, by purchasing used parts (remember you bought a *used* car) from local junkyards and having the work done by small specialized garages, the total amount of your repair losses can be controlled. What may have been an estimated loss of $250 may even be reduced to less than $100 by sharp repair bargaining.

9. Freedom from the "new-car warranty blues." Used-car purchasers are protected from manufacturing defects and deceptive practices under state and federal legislation. There is no "expressed" warranty made by the manufacturer that can restrict the hapless consumer's right to damages. In fact, the courts have ruled that the manufacturer of a product is liable for the damages caused by that product even if the person injured was not the original purchaser. As for misleading statements or "puffery," as many advertising men like to call the practice, the federal government takes a dim view of anyone using the technique to sell products (especially cars) to unsuspecting, gullible consumers.

So, the typical used-car buyer is protected by a multitude of federal and state laws that go far beyond whatever protection may be offered by the standard new-car guarantee. Furthermore, the used-car purchaser does not have to conform to any arbitrary rules or service guidelines in order to benefit from the legal warranty. It is interesting to see how many new-car owners are fighting cases in court against car manufacturers who have not satisfied them with their new-car warranty. In such cases, the consumers invariably ask that the court apply the much stricter legal *implied* warranty rather than accept the manufacturer's defense that the manufacturer's *expressed* warranty wipes out any further legal protection from damages caused by a defective car.

10. Ecological benefits. What could be more ecologically sound than the recycling of old automobiles? Of course the new-car industry would experience a tremendous slump, but that type of shock may be what the industry needs in order to build better vehicles or further diversify into constructing mass-transit components. There would still be a constant supply of used cars because the new-car industry would be heavily supported by the leasing of company cars and the rental-car industry.

11. Freedom in choosing repairs. Used-car owners are not *required* to service their vehicles every 3000–6000 miles at a franchised dealership or to use factory-approved parts installed by a mechanic using a factory-approved flat rate book to estimate repair costs. Used cars can be repaired anywhere. You are not a captive customer of the manufacturer's dealership chain. You also have the freedom not to repair the car if you choose.

12. You can be better informed about a used car. Before buying a used car, the inquiring consumer can find the answers to the following questions: What is the rate of depreciation? How many times has the car been recalled for safety-related defects? Is the vehicle vulnerable to premature rusting? Are parts easily available? Do similar models have a history of costly performance-related defects for that year? (Vega and

Austin Marina owners take note.) What does an independent mechanical inspection disclose about the car's future reliability? If you ask these same questions of a new-car salesman the chances are that they will not be answered.

13. Availability of experienced mechanics. Usually it takes mechanics a few years to learn how to repair the new cars that have been redesigned by the manufacturers. For example, the GM diesels and X-body Citation, Omega, Phoenix, and Skylark models are still too new on the market for mechanics to have sufficient experience to quickly and inexpensively diagnose and correct their defects. Motorists who bought these cars new are still regretting their decision.

14. Litigation easier in lower courts. Most small-claims courts have a jurisdictional limit around $3000. Since most used cars are purchased for less than this amount, any dispute between buyer and seller can be settled within a few months, without lawyers or excessive court costs.

15. Less psychological stress. A used car is pre-dented, pre-rusted, and pre-bumped. So there is little sleep lost over that first dent, rust hole, or fender-bender collision.

There will always be a market for new cars; however, the wise consumer will consider all of these points before deciding on a new-car purchase.

CHOOSING THE RIGHT TIME

Used cars are seldom sold in the winter months of December through March. Car salesmen are hungry for customers and used cars generally show their worst characteristics: no starts, defective heating and defrosting systems, poor suspensions, etc., during this time of the year. It is precisely for these reasons that the smart used-car buyer should shop at this time of the year for real used-car bargains.

One danger in buying a used car in the winter months is that many of the body defects can be concealed by snow or dirt. A good independent inspection by another garage should verify if there is any serious corrosion or accident damage to the sheet metal or the frame of the car. Used cars sold by private individuals should be inspected just as thoroughly before purchase during the winter months.

CHOOSING THE SELLER

Everybody sells used cars, from the federal government to your next-door neighbor. Each sales agency has its own reasons for selling and specific conditions that must be fulfilled for each sales transaction. Guarantees and cash requirements may also vary among different types of sellers.

Private sales. These are the private want ads placed in newspapers, on bulletin boards, and carried through the community grapevine. Prices are usually more than reasonable, the cars have been well maintained, and the seller is not experienced in deception. Two disadvantages with this type of seller is that credit or financing is unavailable from the seller, and there may be no expressed guarantee as to the performance of the vehicle. It may also be possible that the car has been stolen or is owned by a lending institution. Despite these disadvantages, however, the private sale is still the best place to pick up a good, reliable used car at a reasonable price.

Government auctions. Once in a great while, the government will auction off a variety of vehicles, including some jeeps. However, these auctions are so well advertised in advance that the average used-car buyer has little opportunity in outbidding the many professional auction followers who flock to these events. Many vehicles sold at government auctions may never have been used and may be still in their packing crates. However, they, as well as all the other equipment, are not guaranteed. All sales are made in cash and there is little opportunity to inspect the merchandise. Prices may be artificially inflated by an overzealous crowd. In general, government auctions are fun to watch but risky ventures if you don't really know what you are buying.

Commercial automobile auctions. These auctions are frequented by professional car dealers who hope to pick up some cheap cars that can be cheaply reconditioned and then sold at inflated prices. There are no guarantees, cash is required, and prices, like quality, are apt to be low. A minimum inspection of the used cars on display is allowed, but the vehicles cannot leave the display area. Commercial automobile auctions, like the stock market, can wipe out the small, neophyte investor.

Rental and leased car sales. If there are no good used cars available from private owners, then the next best deal might be the purchase of a used car from one of the major car-rental firms. National rental companies such as Hertz (Ford), Avis (Chrysler), and National (General Motors) offer used cars in most of the major cities throughout the United States.

Rental cars that are being unloaded upon the used-car market usually have seen about one year's service and registered about 30,000 miles yearly, depending upon whether they have been rented or leased. The cars are generally well maintained, sell for about 10 percent more than the listed wholesale price, and are sold with a strong guarantee. Many of the car lots selling used rental cars will also provide buyers with a complete history of a car's use and allow an independent inspection of the car's mechanical components by a qualified mechanic of the buyer's choice.

There are a few risks, however, in buying used rental cars from the major rental companies. Since the car has been driven by as many as one hundred drivers, it is possible that the car has been used by many inexperienced, immature, and abusive drivers. Drivers of this sort can cause the strongest car to fall quickly into disrepair.

It is also quite possible to get cheated by rental companies selling used cars. And bigness bears no relation to honesty, either. For example, Hertz recently admitted cheating customers in the selling and repairing of some of its used cars in its Alexandria, Virginia, outlet after the Washington-based Center for Auto Safety exposed the practice. A Hertz spokesman in New York assured the consumer group that steps would be taken to prevent other customers from getting falsified information about cars that had been in crashes, or that had not been repaired properly. Hertz also promised to verify that all cars' service records were accurate.

Nevertheless, no matter who sells a rental car, an independent mechanical examination should be performed before purchase.

Repossessed cars. A repossessed car may be sold by a finance company or bank anxious to recoup its losses. Financing is available, an independent mechanical inspection is usually permitted, and prices can be very reasonable. The biggest problem with repossessed cars is that they have often been abused by their financially troubled owners. Sometimes, the full extent of the abuse these cars have taken cannot be ascertained in one brief garage examination. Before buying a repossessed car, try to find out something about the previous owner and what care was taken of the vehicle. A call to the regional office of the manufacturer will usually provide some clues.

Franchised new-car dealer. New-car dealers get many of their used cars as tradeins from purchasers of new cars. They also get used cars from auto auctions, from rental car sales, and from the street. Thus, there is no real assurance that a franchised new-car dealer will sell good used cars that had been traded in on newer models.

Used cars bought from franchised new-car dealers usually cost $300–$500 more than they would sell for privately. New-car dealers explain that this price markup is the result of reconditioning costs, guarantee costs, and overhead expenses. Financing is available, cars are sometimes permitted to be examined by an independent garage, and there is a much wider choice of models to choose from. Another advantage in dealing with a franchised new-car dealer is that repair facilities are available for warranty repairs. From a purely legalistic point of view, new-car dealers selling used cars are often more financially solvent so there is a better chance of getting paid should a court judgment be won against the firm.

A good, reliable used car can be found at a new-car dealer's lot, but the price may be no bargain and the car will still have to be carefully inspected before purchase.

Independent used-car dealers. Many of the franchised new-car dealers continually accuse independent used-car dealers of giving the automobile industry a bad name through their deceptive advertising and dishonest sales practices. Much of this criticism is true. Yet it is just as true that new-car dealers have also been responsible for the dishonesty prevalent in the automobile industry through their dishonest dealings as documented in the introduction to this guide. The independent used-car dealers are just a reflection of the everyday deceptive activities of many new-car dealers.

Independent used-car dealers offer easy credit, advertise low prices, and offer a variety of used-car models. They usually are marginal operations that are not financially stable and do not have repair facilities with which to honor their warranties. Their used cars may be of doubtful quality, and mechanical testing by another garage may be discouraged on the pretext that there is inadequate insurance or that there are no tags to transport the car off the lot.

Certain used-car dealers use their customers' desire to get a good used car for practically nothing to their own advantage. The search for the perfect used car for a couple of hundred dollars holds an endless fascination for some used-car buyers; but as with most other goods, you get what you pay for, and that "bargain" may bring you nothing but headaches.

Using the Want Ads

Whether you are buying or selling, the used-car want ads can be invaluable. The automobile-exchange pages of your local newspaper will quickly give you a clear idea of what's available in your area—and how much it will cost. There are a few basic pointers to be kept in mind, though, in order to use the want ads most effectively.

Most important, keep away from hyped-up or come-on advertising. An ad that screams in big, bold type: "SHARP! MUST SEE TO BELIEVE!" does not inspire confidence. Stick with the more sober ads that give the information you need without the hoopla. Steer clear of anything that strikes you as suspicious, and be cautious of such catch-all phrases as "mechanic's special," which is to a car what "handyman's special" is to a house and can mean almost everything. Don't be taken in. Call and ask questions. If the answers you get are evasive—or if you don't get any answers at all—you'll know to look elsewhere.

The most effective used-car want ads give all the basic information including make, model, year, mileage, optional features, the price you are asking, and whether this price is firm or negotiable. The ad should also give a number where you can be reached.

Below are some examples of used-car ads that have been well prepared and would be likely to get good results:

> Chevy '79 Caprice, 4-dr, 18,000 miles, a/c,
> am/fm cass, $4600. Call 555-0011 wkends.
> Pontiac Grand Prix '77, orig. owner, 40,000
> mi, ps, pb, asking $3900. Days 555-9580.
> BMW 320i 1980, sunroof, a/c, stereo, excellent
> cond, $11,700 firm. Wkdays 555-7255.
> Buick '78 Regal, 2-dr maroon w/matching int,
> vinyl roof, all pwr, lo mi, excl cond. $4895.
> Dealer 555-6228.

The last ad above was placed by a dealer, not a private owner, and the fact that he identifies himself as such is a point in his favor, although the phrase "lo mi" is a little vague.

Used-car want ads, like other classifieds, make heavy use of abbreviations, and you should familiarize yourself with these shorthand terms before placing an ad or answering one.

> a/c: air conditioning
> am/fm cass: AM/FM radio plus cassette deck
> auto: automatic transmission
> 4-spd man: four-speed manual transmission
> OD: overdrive
> ps: power steering
> pb: power brakes
> all pwr: other power features in addition to power brakes and power steering—i.e., power windows, power locks, and perhaps power seats as well
> buckt: bucket seats
> cruise: cruise control
> tilt: tilt steering wheel

In addition, many ads nowadays list how many miles to the gallon the car gets, both city and highway.

Used-Car Rackets: The Tricks of the Trade

As long as used cars are bought and sold there is going to be a considerable amount of trading carried on to determine the price of the used car being sold. But to be sure you're not getting the short end of the bargaining stick, you should be aware of pricing tactics.

One of the purposes of this guide is to inform you of the more common used-car rackets that are practiced by dealers and by some private sellers.

It would be impossible to list all the fraudulent sales techniques employed. As soon as the public is alerted to one scheme, other more elaborate frauds may be used by enterprising salesmen. Nevertheless, there are some basic fraudulent practices that have been used so often that they have become legendary. Some of these practices are:

Failing to declare full purchase price. Purchasers of used cars are told by the salesman that they can save the amount of sales tax to be paid if they put a lower selling price on the contract. So, a car selling for $2000 is declared to have been purchased for only $1000. The buyer, therefore, can save as much as 8 percent of the sales tax on $1000, or about $80. But what if the car turns out to be a lemon, or the salesman has falsified the model year mileage, or mechanical condition of the vehicle? Generally, nothing will happen because the salesman will then tell the hapless buyer that he will refund the customer's *full purchase price* that is indicated on the contract, namely, $1000. Even if the buyer wanted to take the dealer to court, it is very unlikely, say some lawyers, that any more than the contract price would be awarded. It is also possible that both parties could be prosecuted by the state tax authorities for making a false declaration to avoid paying state sales taxes. All this trouble can occur, just because the buyer is trying to save about $80 in taxes. Is it worth it?

The wrong model year. Thousands of used cars, trucks motorcycles and mobile homes on the market are being sold for the wrong model year. In fact, model year "updating" or "reclassification" has been used by many car companies to pass off old, unsold stock as the latest model. Generally, it is consumers who bought their cars new who have been caught by this new car fraud. Now, however, these same vehicles are being sold as used cars by dealers who are well aware of the fact that these cars are "reclassified" models and that registering them for the wrong model year does not necessarily make them that model year. Private owners may also knowingly or unknowingly pass off these incorrectly registered cars to unsuspecting used-car purchasers.

So far, a majority of import car companies have been convicted of updating their cars' model year. Most of these convictions have been before the small-claims courts. The companies that have been involved in this updating fraud have been: Nissan (Datsun), Toyota, Mazda, Chrysler (Colt), Renault, Citroën, Fiat, British Leyland, and BMW.

The best way to protect yourself from model year fraud is to inspect the plate indicating the date of manufacture located on the inside door pillar on the driver's side of the vehicle. It is a federal crime to remove the plate. Another indication of the model year of an imported vehicle is the pollution-control sticker that is usually affixed somewhere in the engine compartment. This sticker will show what model year pollution-control equipment the car has and how the car should be tuned in accordance with the pollution-control equipment. The model year can also be determined by examining the date sticker on the seatbelts. Each seatbelt has a mandatory sticker showing the date of manufacture. Seatbelts are usually manufactured a few months before the car is completely assembled at the factory. Don't jump to the conclusion you have bought a reclassified car because the tail lights or side marker lamps may show a difference of several years. These lamps are often built years in advance and do not change that often.

The federally-required date-of-manufacture compliance plate should read September or later for cars of the current model year. Plates that show the car was manufactured 7/72 or 2/72 are probably updated models because the model year usually doesn't change until September of the year they are introduced. One of the few exceptions to this rule would be certain domestic cars that may be introduced *for the first time* in late May or early June. This is what happened with the first Mustang and Maverick models when they were put on the market.

A good rule of thumb is to suspect every foreign car of being updated unless the manufacturer's plate shows that the car has been built after August. Don't buy any car that does not have this plate.

Car dealers placing "private" want ads. Dealers will hire men and women to use their home addresses and telephone numbers to sell their used cars. Sometimes a salesman will be encouraged to take a particular used car home and sell it. By far the most extensive use of this trick has been by groups of professional salespersons who buy hundreds of cars from dealers and auto auctions at wholesale prices and then place a number of ads in the local papers selling these same cars as privately owned vehicles. Most new-car dealers get very angry when one of these teams hits town. Unfortunately, these dealers do not get angry enough, because they continue to sell used cars at wholesale prices to these people. A careful buyer can spot this fraud by asking to see the vehicle's registration, the initial sales contract, or some routine repair orders that every motorist accumulates during the ownership of a car.

You can also spot a professional car dealer in the want-ad section of the newspaper by checking whether one telephone number is repeated in many different ads. For example, it is obvious in the following used-car want ads that Mr. Smith and Mr. Jones work together as professional used-car salesmen:

> Mercury Capri 1980, 6-cyl, standard/OD, 3-dr
> hatchback, am/fm $5000. Mr. Smith,
> Agent 555-2164
> Mercury Bobcat 1977 exc cond, auto trans,
> am/fm, $2700. Mr. Jones, Agent 555-2164

Fortunately, both Mr. Smith and Mr. Jones were required by the newspaper to state that they were acting as an "agent" for a professional used-car dealer and, therefore, did not mislead the public with their advertising. Many newspapers do not have this rule so it is best to be on guard.

"Free-exchange" privilege. Used-car dealers get a lot of sales mileage out of this deceptive practice. The average consumer feels protected against buying a "lemon" because the dealer offers to exchange the newly purchased car for any other in stock if the buyer is not perfectly satisfied. What often happens, though, is that the dealer will not have any other cars selling for the same low price and will thus demand a cash bonus for the exchange. Another possibility is that the dealer may have nothing but "lemons" in stock, so no matter which car is finally chosen, the buyer still gets stuck.

"Money-back" guarantee. Once again the purchaser feels safe in buying a used car with this kind of guarantee because what could be more honest than a money-back guarantee? Dealers using this guarantee to deceive customers will often charge exorbitant handling charges, rental fees, or mechanical repair costs to customers who have bought one of these vehicles and then returned it afterward. Some of the "special fees" that may be charged by a crooked dealer using this trick can run as high as $300–$500. To avoid this fraud, read the sales contract carefully.

"50/50" guarantee. A 50/50 guarantee means that the dealer will pay one-half the repair costs over a limited period of time. This is a fair proposition if the dealer does not insist that the vehicle be brought to his garage in order to benefit from the guarantee. What then may happen is that the dealer will inflate the repair costs to double their actual worth and write up a bill for that amount. The buyer winds up paying the full price of the warranty repairs that would probably have been much cheaper at an independent garage. The best kind of used-car warranty is 100 percent for 30 days with full coverage for parts and labor.

"Repossessed" cars. Any car that has been bought or transferred to a third party has been "repossessed." Actually, this term is thrown about by car dealers who hope to lure customers into their showroom so they

can start working up a high-pressure sales pitch to make the buyer believe the car is a bargain.

Most repossessed cars, if they have been repossessed by a financing company, are about the worst type of car one can buy. It stands to reason that if the vehicle's owner could not afford to pay off the car, he or she also couldn't afford to maintain it. In fact, experience shows that many automobile owners who find they are without cash to pay their debts will often run their car into the ground to spite the finance company that has been hassling them to meet their loan payments.

Stay away from "repossessed" cars.

"As is" cars. Buying a car "as is" means that you are aware of the mechanical defects and are prepared to accept the responsibility for any damages or injuries caused by the vehicle and that all costs to fix it up shall be borne by yourself. The courts have held that the "as is" clause must be interpreted in light of the seller's true intent. That is: was there an attempt to deceive the buyer by including this clause? or, did the buyer really know what the "as is" clause could do to his future legal rights? It has also been held that verbal representations, "parole evidence," made by the seller as to the fine quality of the used car but never written into the formal contract, may also be considered by the court.

Odometer tampering. It is often too dangerous for the dealer to turn back the mileage, so many independent "reconditioning" outfits are hired to pick up the car or visit the dealership where the odometer is given a thorough "reconditioning."

Until federal and state laws are enforced and convictions result in severe penalties to anyone engaging in this practice (federal law allows citizens to sue for *triple* damages plus lawyer and court costs), the best protection from the fraud is to take the following steps:

1. Demand that the dealer put the mileage figure on the contract.
2. Ask for the name and address of the previous owner.
3. Ask for old repair receipts, work orders, or warranty repair statements.

When dealing with a private seller, it would be smart to demand that the same requirements be met. After all, anyone can turn back a car's mileage, no matter what the model year.

Misrepresentation of a used car. Used cars can be misrepresented in a variety of ways. A used taxi may be represented as having belonged to a little old lady. A mechanically defective car that has been rebuilt from several major accidents may have sawdust in its transmission to muffle the "clunks," a heavy oil in the motor to stifle the "clanks," and cheap retread tires to eliminate the "thumps." All of these practices are fraudulent and may lead to the dealer's being prosecuted for civil or criminal fraud. The best protection against this type of "dirty trick" is a complete mechanical verification by an independent mechanic before purchasing the vehicle.

Private Sales Rackets

A lot of space in this guide has been used to describe how used-car dealers can cheat the average uninformed used-car buyer. Of course, private individuals also are capable of taking advantage of used-car buyers. Generally, the typical used-car crook who is not associated with a professional sales team will use some of the following deceptive practices.

Used cars with finance owing. Because he can't keep up loan payments, this crook will sell the car through the want ads of the local newspaper and then skip town. By the time the buyer is aware that the car has not been paid for, most legal recourses are ineffective. The lending institution then may offer the buyer the privilege of purchasing the car again — from them, since it is now their property. In effect, the unwary customer may end up buying the same car twice.

This racket can be stopped if buyers demand proof of purchase and payment from any individual who offers to sell a used car for an incredibly low price. Check the sales contract to determine which finance company or bank granted the original auto loan and check with them to see if the loan had been repaid. Place a call to the Department of Motor Vehicles to check if the vehicle is registered in the seller's name. Finally, call up the original dealer to determine whether there are any outstanding claims against the vehicle.

Stolen Cars. Stolen cars are almost always sold through private individuals. Car dealers have found the risks too great. Potential profits are more appealing when they cheat consumers by the use of the pen rather than engaging in activities that carry heavy criminal penalties. The best defense against buying a stolen car is to check with the police, the Department of Motor Vehicles, and the original selling dealer on the current status of the vehicle. All of this scrutiny can take a day or so but it will pay off in the long run.

Mileage Turnbacks. When buying a used car from a private seller, be suspicious if the mileage registers less than 15,000 miles for each year the car has been in use. Ask for repair receipts, warranty record, or check with the manufacturer as to when last warranty repairs were made. Remember, the mileage is never as important a factor as how the vehicle was driven. A car with only 30,000 miles can be ready for the scrap heap while the same vehicle, if it is well maintained, may be good for at least 150,000 miles.

CHOOSING THE CAR

Personal Used-Car Inspection

The personal nonprofessional inspection of a used car by a potential purchaser means much more than just kicking the tires and slamming the doors. A careful, informed inspection of a used car can usually discover many of the car's most serious defects. Remember that no used car should be bought without having an inspection made by an independent mechanic; however, some simple checks can be made personally by carrying out the following:

Interior inspection.
1. Look for excessive wear of the seats, dash, accelerator pedal, brakes, armrests, and roof lining.
2. Check the dash for radio mounting holes (police or taxi) and check the roof lining for same. Is the radio tuned to local stations?
3. Do the doors open easily and close tightly? Loose fits or defective doors can indicate that the car was in an accident.
4. Turn the steering wheel and listen for unusual noises or watch for excessive steering wheel play (more than an inch).
5. Test the emergency brake with car parked on a hill.
6. Inspect the seatbelts (post-1966 models only). See if the webbing is in good condition and, on some Ford models, make sure the seatbelts are long enough to be fastened.
7. Make sure the door latches and locks are in good working

order. If the rear doors have no handles or locks, or if they have just been replaced, the car may have been a police patrol car.
8. Try out the seat adjustments to see if the seating position can be moved into all the positions intended by the manufacturer. Look under the seats to make sure the seat runners are functioning as they should.
9. Check the head support (post-1970 cars) for ease of adjustment and see if the apparatus blocks rear vision.
10. Peel back the floor rugs and check the metal floor for signs of rust or dampness. While crawling around on the car's floor, look for any pieces of paper or documents that may provide additional information about the car's present condition or past history.

Exterior inspection.
1. If the car has been repainted recently, check the quality of the paint job by inspecting the engine and trunk compartments and the inside door panels. Make sure this is done on a clear day so that any wavy paint irregularities will show.
2. Inspect the paint for tiny bubbles. This may mean that the car has been poorly primed before painting or that it is rusting prematurely.
3. Have the bumpers been damaged or recently repaired? Remember, new bumpers usually last far longer than the six months to one year that rechromed bumpers last. Check the bumper supporting struts.
4. See if the hood and rear trunk lid close and open without difficulty. Make sure they both look properly aligned.
5. Test the shock absorbers by pushing hard on a corner of the vehicle. If the car bounces around like a ship at sea, the shocks could need replacing.
6. Look at the muffler and exhaust pipe to detect premature wear, or displacement from a low-impact collision (this could channel deadly carbon monoxide into the passenger area).
7. Check for tire wear. Don't forget the spare. Be suspicious if all tires are new. The car could have serious frame damage or suspension problems. Ask if tires are retreads. (See illustration).

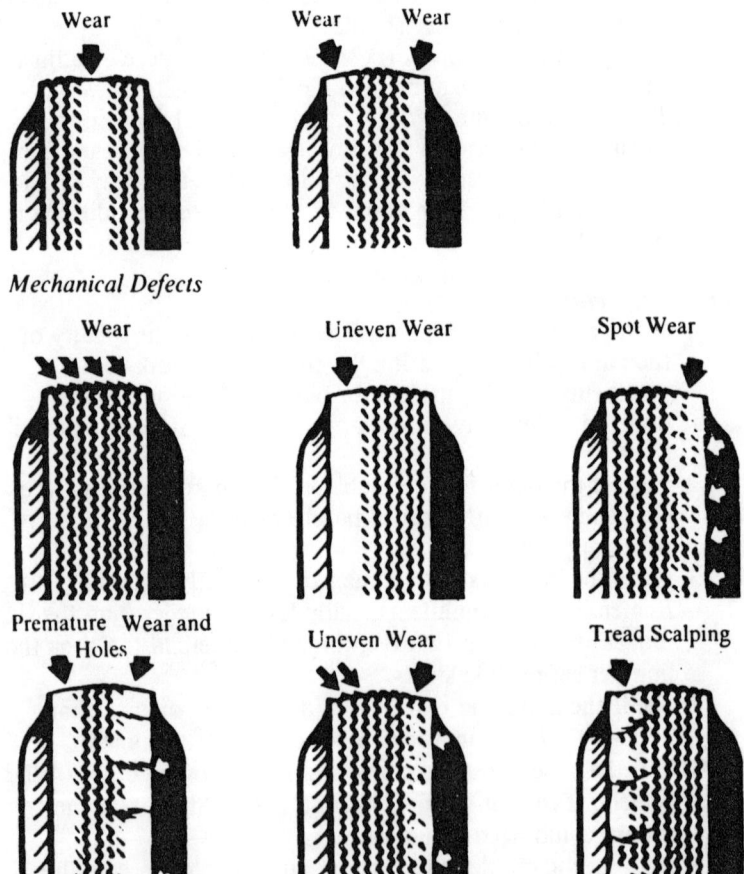

FIGURE 1: COMMON TIRE PROBLEMS

8. Make sure the rear trunk contains a spare tire, a jack, and tools necessary for changing a tire. Also look for premature rusting in the side wheel wells and for water in the trunk area.
9. Knock gently on the body of the car where rusting usually appears first. Places like the front fenders, door bottoms, rear wheel wells, and station wagon rear doors are likely areas. Even if these areas have been repaired with plastic, lead, metal plating or fiberglass, once rusting starts it is difficult to stop.
10. Look how the car sits. If one side or end is higher than the other, it could mean that the suspension system is defective.
11. Ask the seller to turn on the headlights (low and high beam), turn signals, parking lights, emergency blinking lights, and ask him to blow the horn. From the rear, check that the brake lights, back-up lights, turn indicators, tail lights, and license plate light are all functioning.

Road test.
1. Start the vehicle and listen for unusual noises.
2. With the motor running, check out all dashboard controls such as the windshield wipers, heater and defroster, and the radio.
3. Listen to the motor while car is in idle. If the motor stalls or races a simple adjustment may fix the trouble. Loud clanking noises or a low oil pressure could mean potentially expensive defects.
4. While in neutral, push down on the accelerator abruptly. If blue smoke comes from the exhaust a minor adjustment of the motor or carburetor may be necessary. Black smoke may mean major engine repairs.
5. Shift the transmission into drive with the motor still idling. The vehicle should creep slowly forward without stalling or speeding. Listen for unusual noises when the transmission is engaged. Cars with manual transmissions should engage as soon as the clutch has shifted gears. Transmission slipping or stalling could require the replacement of the clutch plate.
6. When the transmission has been shifted into drive and while the motor is idling apply the emergency handbrake to stop

the car. If the motor is not racing and the brake is in good condition, the car should stop.
7. Accelerate to 30 miles an hour while slowly moving through all gears. Listen for transmission noises.
8. At 30 miles an hour, step lightly on the brakes. The brake response should be immediate and equal for all wheels.
9. In a deserted shopping center or parking lot, test the vehicle's steering and suspension by driving in figure eights at low speeds.
10. While driving at a moderate speed of 20 miles an hour, take both hands off the steering wheel to see whether the vehicle veers from one side to the other. Once again alignment or suspension could be defective. (When conducting this test, make sure that the highway is clear of traffic and pedestrians.)
11. Test the suspension by driving over some rough terrain.
12. Stop the car at the foot of a small hill and see if the car can climb the hill without difficulty.
13. Accelerate on an expressway from 0 to 60 miles an hour. It should take no longer than 20 seconds for most cars to reach 60 miles an hour from a standing start.
14. Drive through a tunnel with the windows open. Try to detect any unusual sounds coming from the car. (Seller's sobbings excepted.)
15. After driving the car, test the transmission once again by shifting from drive to neutral to reverse. Listen for clunking sounds coming from the transmission when it is engaged.
16. With the car stopped and running in the park position, open the hood to check for any leakage of fluid. The check for fluid leakage should have been done before the car was first driven away and should also be repeated 10 minutes after the motor has been shut off. Don't leave the car unattended with motor running while standing in back of vehicle. Over 16 million 1972–79 Ford vehicles have transmissions that may slip from park to reverse and run you over.

Many of these testing procedures will undoubtedly turn up some defects that may be major or minor. If such is the case, an independent mechanic should be told which areas are suspect and additional time should be spent in double-checking those areas.

Independent Garage Inspection

An independent mechanic will verify most used cars for less than $50. For the price, the following mechanical components should be looked at:

Carburetor	Suspected leaks
Motor compression test	Wheel alignment
Wiring	Exhaust system
Brakes	Ball joints
Power steering, power brakes	Chassis corrosion
Radiator	or misalignment
Water pump and generator	Headlight alignment
Battery	Anti-freeze checked
Transmission fluid	Tire wear measured

A good garage mechanic should do all of the necessary work within two hours. Any special checks could take longer.

Diagnostic Clinics

Oil company affiliated diagnostic clinics are not recommended for motorists wishing to verify the mechanical condition of a used car. Many of these clinics also have repair bays that place them in a conflict of interest when making their diagnoses. Exxon once even had a salary policy that gave their clinic employees a bonus based upon the parts that were replaced on cars coming in for service. The only diagnostic clinic that could be useful would be one that did not do any automotive repairs. If such a clinic exists nearby, it may be used as long as it is equipped to carry out the mechanical verification that is necessary.

How Long Should a Part Last?

Many times, used-car dealers will repair a defective part only to have that same defect reappear a few thousand miles or a few months later when the warranty has expired. Motorists who do not have an expert handy to challenge the dealer's opinion that the defect is not a defect at all but is normal wear and tear may find the following special study of interest.

How Much Will a Part Cost?

Table 3 gives an estimated guide to selected parts costs. Use this guide to deduct the costs of parts from a used car's selling price.

TABLE 2
Part Life

Repair	Average Repair Interval in Miles
Brake System	
Brake drum, replace	300,000
Brake drum, turn	29,300
Drum brake linings, renew	38,800
Wheel cylinder, rebuild	30,850
Master cylinder, rebuild	102,900
Steering and Suspension	
Ball joint, replace	128,700
Shock absorber, replace	70,720
Wheel bearing, replace	100,020
Wheel balance	13,422
Front-end alignment	55,096
Power steering gear, recondition	over 100,000
Power steering hose, replace	over 100,000
Exhaust System	
Tail-pipe, replace	51,794
Muffler, replace	46,596
Exhaust pipe, replace	131,095
Ignition System	
Cable set, replace	143,300
Spark plugs (set), replace or clean	16,248
Tuneup	16,709
Points and condenser, replace	18,024
Retiming	66,760
Fuel System	
Carburetor, replace	78,151
Fuel pump, replace	102,040
Fuel filter, replace	39,635
Air cleaner, replace	26,809
Visibility	
Sealed beam, replace	28,105
Aim headlights	62,735
Speedometer cable, replace	over 100,000
Windshield wiper motor, replace	over 100,000

SOURCE: Booz-Allen Applied Research, Inc., *Maintainability and Repairability of Vehicles in Use,* Final Report, June 1971, Volume 2, pp. 3-29, presented as evidence before the United States Senate Subcommittee on Antitrust and Monopoly studying the automobile repair industry, June 1968-1969.

TABLE 3
Part Cost

	1975	New	Rebuilt	Used
Motor	GM (350)	$1500.00	$550.00	$450.00
	Ford (302)	$1700.00	$450.00	$350.00
	Duster (318)	$1500.00	$674.00	$400.00
Transmission	GM	$ 800.00	$310.00	$125.00
	Ford	$ 900.00	$257.00	$125.00
	Duster	$ 600.00	$240.00	$125.00
Alternator	GM	$ 145.20	$ 46.95	$ 20.00
	Ford	$ 164.90	$ 30.00	$ 20.00
	Chrysler	$ 105.00	$ 33.95	$ 20.00
Starter	GM	$ 200.55	$ 36.40	$ 20.00
	Ford	$ 150.00	$ 33.75	$ 20.00
	Duster	$ 145.00	$ 47.75	$ 20.00
Windshield wiper motor	GM	$ 150.05	$ 30.00	$ 20.00
	Ford	$ 120.45		$ 20.00
	Duster	$ 120.00		$ 20.00
Door	Chevrolet	$ 300.00		$125.00
	Fairlane	$ 250.25		$125.00
	Duster	$ 200.00		$125.00

The Quality of Servicing

Used-car purchasers can profit from the experiences of new car owners who have reported the quality of servicing of different models of cars to the federal government and other private consumer protection agencies. This service rating was compiled by the Automobile Protection Association. Remember, some companies that have been rated poorly or have a generally poor dealer body may have *some* exceptionally fine and honest dealers.

TABLE 4
Dealer's After-sale Service

Make	Quality of Service	Adequacy of Repairs	Availability of Repairs	Fairness of Charge	Courtesy of Dealer
AMC	A	A	-	+ +	A
Audi	A	A	-	A	+
BMW	+ +	+ +	-	-	+ +
Buick	+	A	A	—	A
Cadillac	+ +	A	A	A	A
Chevrolet	—	—	A	—	-
Chrysler	—	—	—	—	A
Citroën	A	A	—	—	—
Datsun	A	-	-	-	A
Dodge	—	—	A	—	A
Fiat	—	—	—	—	—
Ford	A	A	A	-	A
GMC	A	A	A	A	A
Honda	+	+	A	+	+
International	-	-	-	A	A
Jeep	-	-	-	A	+
Lincoln	A	A	+	A	A
Mazda	—	—	-	—	A
Mercedes-Benz	-	-	A	-	A
Mercury	A	A	A	-	A
Oldsmobile	A	-	+	-	-
Opel	-	-	-	A	A
Peugeot	-	-	-	-	-
Plymouth	-	-	-	-	-
Pontiac	A	A	A	A	A
Porsche	+ +	+	A	A	A
Renault	-	A	+	A	A
Saab	-	A	—	-	+
Subaru	+ +	+ +	—	A	A
Toyota	A	A	A	—	A
Volkswagen	+ +	+ +	+	+ +	+ +
Volvo	-	—	A	-	-
British Leyland*	—	—	—	-	-

44

*British Leyland products included the Austin, Rover, Triumph, MG, Jaguar.
+ +   Much better than average
+   Better than average
A   Average
-     Worse than average
—   Much worse than average

Bumpers that Bump

A car's vulnerability to damage caused by low-speed collisions is another important characteristic to consider when buying a used car. Since 1973, American automakers have had to comply with the United States government standards that require bumpers to withstand low-speed collision up to 10 miles per hour without transmitting any damage to the vehicle's mechanical components.

Although this standard has forced many car companies to radically redesign their cars, there has not been any overall public benefit derived from the new standard. In fact, the Washington-based Insurance Institute For Highway Safety has been monitoring the situation since 1970, and this group has alleged that the auto industry has made bumpers that absorbed low-speed impacts better, but the savings were not passed on to consumers because the bumpers were more expensive to replace.

The Accessory Jungle

Very few new cars are sold without some gadget included by the salesman who just could not find a stripped-down version of the same model in stock. With compact and subcompact new cars, dealers often use the technique of forcing unnecessary options on new-car buyers to increase profits by another 10 percent. Sometimes, an automobile accessory may give the dealer as much as 50 percent profit. Unfortunately, many new-car purchasers have to take what their dealer claims he has in stock.

In shopping for a good used car, the situation is different. Because of the availability of a variety of used cars, there is a greater selection of cars that are not loaded with unwanted options. Some cars that may offer accessories of a doubtful value can also be purchased for much less than when they were new.

Some of the optional equipment found on used cars is of no value whatsoever. Yet, some private owners or used-car dealers may try to pretend otherwise. The following is an evaluation of some of the optional equipment found on many used cars.

Power brakes. This device is only needed in a car weighing more than 3200 pounds, equipped with an 8-cylinder motor. Elderly or handicapped persons may consider this option necessary. As a car ages, this component may fail and cause a safety hazard or require costly repairs. Don't give more than $50 for this optional feature. Some 1973–1975 Chrysler models have had a considerable amount of difficulty with their power-brake systems.

Power steering. Once again, this is one extra that is only needed in steering large, heavy cars. Many power-steering systems are failure-prone and they often give the driver a false feel of the roadway. Don't pay anything extra for this option if you are buying a compact or subcompact model. For heavier cars, offer $25 for the option. Remember, both power steering and power brakes will reduce gasoline mileage.

Electric windows and electric seats. Many intermediate and luxury cars come equipped with these totally unnecessary and expensive options. As mentioned before, these options can deteriorate within a few years to the point where a mechanic may almost have to tear the car apart to find a poor wiring connection or fix a short-circuit. Don't pay anything extra for this option and if possible, ask for a discount for taking this potential trouble off its owner's hands.

Remote-controlled side mirror. Another Disneyland gadget that is failure-prone and expensive to repair. Learn to stick your hand out of the window and adjust the mirror. This option is worth nothing.

Rustproofing. There is no independent proof that rustproofing actually prevents or retards the premature rusting of automobiles. Nevertheless, it is obvious that some owners feel that a used car that has been rustproofed is a better buy than one that has not. This is not necessarily so, since a rustproofed car may begin rusting prematurely if it was parked in a heated garage during the winter or if the vehicle has a defective design that encourages rusting in areas where most rustproofing compounds cannot reach. It is true, however, that rustproofed cars ride more quietly due to the muffling of road noise by the rustproofing product. Don't pay anything extra for a car that has been rustproofed, unless the owner or rustproofing company will provide you with a guarantee against premature rusting. If such a guarantee is offered, it could be worth as much as $25.

Radio. This is one accessory that is recommended. A simple AM model will provide weather forecasts and traffic bulletins that may prove invaluable for saving driving time or avoiding bad weather conditions. Check the quality of the radio. Sometimes used-car dealers will substitute cheap imitations for the factory-installed radios. This has been especially common with the Delco radios supplied with General Motors cars. An AM radio should be available for $25, while a more sophisticated AM-FM set may cost as much as $75 depending upon quality and condition.

A CB radio is a recommended option primarily because of its potential as a distress-signaling device that can be used for all kinds of driving emergencies. It is impossible to say how much a CB radio should cost since there are so many different types on the market. Before accepting a CB radio option, have the radio appraised by a friend who can check the retail selling price, condition, and verify that all the components are in good working condition.

Sun roof. Unless you plan to drive the car in Florida or other warm areas the advantages of a car equipped with a sun roof are far outweighed by the disadvantages. Owners of cars equipped with a sun roof complain frequently of wind noises, water leaks, and road dust accumulation. It is a worthless option for most northern climates. Where the climate permits its use, the sun roof may be worth as much as $50.

Tires. Radial tires are definitely recommended. However, radial tires manufactured by Goodyear, Firestone, and Uniroyal are not recommended because of reports of premature tread separation which results in catastrophic tire failure. Michelin radials are the preferred choice because of their low tread wear and liberal warranty policies. Each radial tire with average wear is worth about $20 each or $100 for a set of five tires.

Bucket seats. Bucket seats are best suited for bucket bottoms. Ordinary individuals may find this type of seat very uncomfortable. The bucket seat option is worth little on the used-car market except for the bucket seats of some European cars such as Renault which are more comfortable than most. Still, this option is not much of a factor in determining a used-car's value.

Vinyl roofs. Another useless accessory that is expensive to repair. Vinyl roofs have a tendency to crack and peel within a few years. Generally it can cost $200–$230 to repair this kind of damage to a vinyl roof. In addition to damaging easily, vinyl roofs also absorb the sun's rays so that air conditioning may be necessary. Finally, vinyl roofs may require a lot of personal attention because they become dirty quite easily. It is an option that has very little resale value.

Air conditioner. Although an air conditioner may reduce one's fuel economy by as much as 20 percent, many consumers living in hot climates are ready to lose the extra fuel economy in exchange for the benefits of air conditioning. However, air conditioning is not a logical buy in a used car for purchasers in northern climates. The biggest drawback in buying a used car with air conditioning is in trying to find someone competent enough to fix the gizmo and to find parts when the system breaks down. Generally, an air conditioner has very little value on the used-car market, however, in certain areas a car with this system may be worth $100 more than a car without this option. If possible, it is best to steer clear of the air-conditioning option and drive with the windows open instead.

Automatic cruise control. Many automakers provided this option for motorists too lazy to keep their foot on the accelerator for long periods of high-speed driving. The option is worthless because it is failure-prone and expensive to repair.

"Hidden" front headlights. Many cars offer this feature as standard equipment. The Corvette and Opel are two models that used this feature extensively. The "hidden" headlight design is unacceptable for northern climates because of unpredictable temperature changes. Should the mechanism become frozen shut or partially shut, driving could be extremely hazardous. Once again this is a design dictated more by Detroit's stylists than by mechanical engineers. Avoid any models that use this headlight design. Don't pay anything extra for the privilege of breaking down some cold winter night.

Disc brakes. A European innovation that finally caught on in America, disc brakes are a recommended option because of their superior stopping ability and longer life compared to drum brakes of a similar quality. Nevertheless, one of the more persistent problems with disc brakes is their vulnerability to slush and road debris which may cause the premature wear of the disc-brake components. Generally, if a disc-brake system has been well maintained and there are no factory-designed defects (as with the Datsun 240-Z) a disc-brake option is definitely recommended. On used cars, it is worth about $50. Make sure that the system has been inspected for premature wear and that there is a protective plate to keep slush and road debris out.

Battery. The only battery that is optional for northern climates is the heavy-duty battery offered by many new-car manufacturers and parts wholesalers. If a heavy-duty battery has less than one year's use, it can be worth as much as $25, depending upon its condition.

Heavy-duty suspension. Most new-car buyers purchase a car with heavy-duty suspension because they intend to use the car to pull a trailer or to drive over rough terrain. This option is worth little unless the suspension is in good condition, which is rarely the case.

Heavy-duty motor. The days of the eight-cylinder high-performance motor are numbered. Rarely is such a powerful, gas-wasting motor necessary for the everyday needs of an average motorist. Perhaps motorists who have to pull a trailer may require a high-performance motor, but for most drivers, a small six-cylinder engine should perform just as well. The eight-cylinder motor is unnecessary for most driving needs and will be very costly in repairs, insurance premiums, and gasoline consumption. However, some of the early small six-cylinder and 231 CID V-6 and eight-cylinder 305 CID V-8 motors from GM have serious crankshaft and camshaft defects.

Catalytic converter. The Environmental Protection Agency asked the major automakers to clean up the air and the response from the domestic automobile manufacturers was a Frankenstein-like mechanical apparatus called the catalytic converter. Although it is standard equipment, there is very little that is positive that can be said about this pollution-control device. All that can be said is that the mechanism does not do its job and is extremely costly to replace. It has the following disadvantages that the major automobile manufacturers fail to mention:

- It may reduce gas mileage considerably.
- It could cause a fire by increasing exhaust system temperatures.

- It may cause nausea because of foul-smelling odors coming from the exhaust system.
- It could cost as much as $150–$200 to replace after the 5-year emissions warranty expires.
- It requires unleaded gasoline that is not available in many urban and rural areas and may cost 3 to 5 cents more than regular leaded gas.
- It is likely to be dropped as soon as alternative pollution-control systems are found.

As a result of all the serious problems caused by the catalytic converter system, motorists are urged to choose used cars with more conventional pollution-control devices. Obviously, a used car equipped with a catalytic converter system will not command as high a price on the used-car market as one that has a conventional system for controlling pollutants.

Courtesy lights. Automatic switches that turn on the car's lights when the doors or trunk are open are of doubtful value. They needlessly complicate a car's wiring and can be costly to repair. Cost is variable.

Electric antenna. Another useless, expensive gadget that easily short-circuits. Cost is usually figured in a complete trim package.

Master-locking switch. A safety feature that is useful when carrying children.

Seatbelts. Many vehicles built before 1966, or specifically exempted by law, may not be equipped with seatbelts. If this is the case, it would be wise to spend $100 to have them installed.

According to a recent study done by the California Highway Patrol, there is "compelling evidence" that seatbelts reduce the severity of traffic accident injury in frontal crashes. Highway Patrol Commissioner Glen Craig admitted that the 1978 study did show that nonusers of seatbelts had *fewer* injuries in rear-end and side-swipe collisions. More than 1715 accidents were analyzed in this study.

Trailer towing options. Although fuel economy is bound to suffer, trailer towing requires a considerable amount of extra equipment in order to be safe and trouble-free. Suspension modifications, heavy-duty power brakes, increased capacity coolant systems for the engine oil, and transmission fluid are particularly important options required when towing a trailer.

Because of the hazards involved, never take a car salesman's advice as to which equipment is necessary without checking first with the manufacturer of the trailer that is to be towed.

Turbocharging. Turbocharging has long been used to give added power to diesel truck engines and sports cars. Both General Motors and Ford, however, have only recently begun selling them as optional equipment, claiming they save fuel as well as give spectacular fuel economy. Unfortunately, such is not the case. For example, the 1979 Buick optional Turbo V-6 engines sold for $600 more than GM's standard engine. This price difference requires huge gasoline savings in order to bring the Turbo's high initial cost into line. But from all reports, the Turbo cannot deliver that kind of fuel economy. In fact, Environmental Protection Agency fuel consumption figures for 1979 vehicles showed that the Turbo Mustang produced a city rating of 18 MPG, as compared with a much more reasonable 21 MPG with the standard Mustang four-cylinder engine. General Motors' Turbo V-6 Regal and Century models performed just as poorly. Both Turbo cars gave a city rating of 17 MPG, as compared with 19 MPG obtained by GM's standard 231 CID V-6 engine.

Turbocharged motors also require premium gasoline to give the maximum boost in a motor's performance. This is especially true of GM's 1978–1980 turbocharged Buicks, Chevrolets, and Pontiacs.

Turbocharged motors are far more complicated in their operation than standard engines. Also, they require parts that may not be readily available in most dealerships, nor in independent garages, for that matter. And should the shaft bearings fail, or the compressor impeller be destroyed by dirt contamination, it would be necessary to rebuild or replace the entire turbocharger system at a cost of $300–$500.

Although early reports from owners of turbocharged vehicles do not show a high incidence of failures, it only takes one to leave a lasting impression on your pocketbook. So why take the chance?

Special "sports package." Sometimes a new-car dealer will sell a consumer some optional equipment that may be completely unnecessary. This is what has happened when you see ordinary vehicles decked out in sports-car trappings. Although many of the sports-car trappings such as a special paint job or special hub caps are purely artificial inducements to pay a higher price for a very ordinary automobile, many private owners sell these cars at a loss without realizing that the radial tires, special suspension, and power brakes could be sold for much more. Check out each used car for its "package" options and bargain for each item individually to arrive at a fair total price. Remember, don't be overly impressed by the initial cost of many new-car options included in a sports package because the price of these options has certainly been inflated at the time of sale and, since that time, the depreciation of these same options has been at least 50 percent or more.

Remember, then, that automobile options are worth much less when they return to the used-car market than when they were first sold to uninformed buyers as new-car options. Nevertheless, there are some used-car options that merit a second look because their prices and availability have become more acceptable with age.

Import or Domestic Model?

There is still a lot of controversy surrounding the relative merits of foreign and domestic cars. Before deciding which car is best, it would be wise to forget all the popular mythology and try to get solid facts.

Almost without exception, foreign-car parts are much more expensive than their domestic equivalent, despite some similar retail prices. A good way to check these prices is to compare prices on certain items one would expect to replace frequently. Exhaust systems, brake pads, body parts, and electrical components are the best indicators. Time permitting, verify replacement costs for major items, such as the transmission and motor, as well.

Servicing also needs to be investigated since this has traditionally been the *bête noire* of the importer in North America. For example, a vehicle can have the best engineering features in the world, but if the servicing is lousy, that vehicle will quickly deteriorate and fall into a lemon category. Volkswagen, Fiat, and Volvo are well aware of this problem and are trying to improve servicing procedures at the dealership level.

Verify how often the vehicle needs to be serviced, and whether that servicing is reliable and inexpensive. Of course, no dealer is going to admit to recurring problems on a particular model and thereby lose a potential sale. So check servicing costs with other car owners driving similar models and be on the lookout for cars showing the dealer's nameplate on the trunk. Ask owners to evaluate the quality of service found at their dealership. It also might be worthwhile to check with fleet owners about the servicing problems they are encountering with their foreign or domestic vehicles. Finally, question closely regional and national automobile consumer-protection groups as to which vehicles receive the most complaints and what mechanical components are the most failure-prone. Remember that most consumer groups need at least six months worth of complaints in order to properly evaluate new cars.

Be wary of dual dealerships that carry several different makes of new cars. These dealers often cannot afford to maintain an adequate inventory of replacement parts.

Median life of passenger cars in Sweden 1978. When the annual compulsory inspection was introduced in 1965, the median life* for passen-

TABLE 5

Median Life for Passenger Cars in the United States and Sweden for the Years 1963–1978

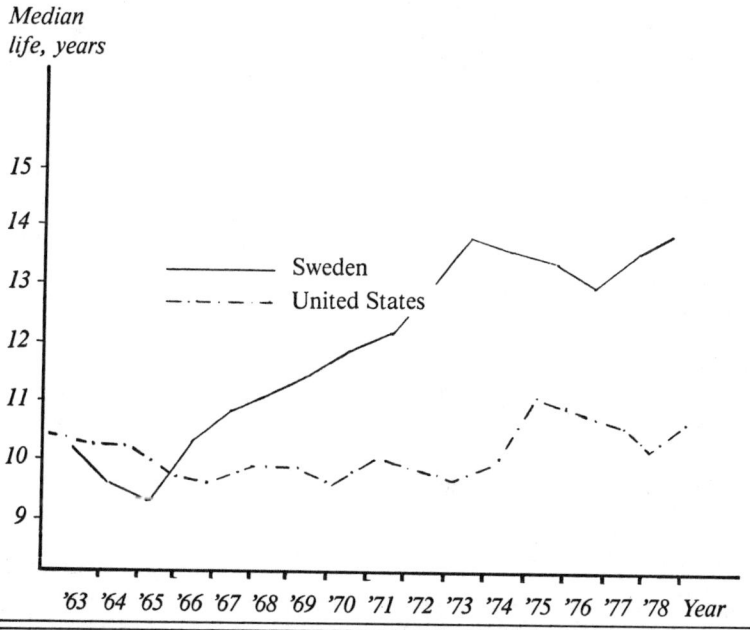

*Median life is the age which 50 percent of the cars surpass and the other 50 percent fail to attain.

ger cars in Sweden had decreased from 13 to 14 years in the fifties to a level just below 10 years.

During the latter part of the sixties and the early seventies the median life increased and amounted to about 14 years in 1973. Since then it has stabilized at this level with only minor deviations.

Another way of measuring the service life of passenger cars is to look at the percentages of the originally registered passenger cars of a certain year model which still remain in traffic. These are shown in Table 6

TABLE 6

THE PERCENTAGES OF THE ORIGINALLY REGISTERED PASSENGER CARS OF THE MAJOR CAR MAKES, YEAR MODELS 1962, 1966 AND 1970, WHICH REMAIN ON THE ROAD AT THE END OF 1978

Car make	Percentage remaining of year model		
	1962 (about 16 years old)	1966 (about 12 years old)	1970 (about 8 years old)
All passenger cars	27	62	94
BMC	16	37	88
BMW	13	49	94
Citroën	16	49	94
DKW/Audi	10	42	91
Fiat	12	38	82
Ford	16	47	91
Mercedes-Benz	30	75	97
Opel	16	53	92
Peugeot	19	42	85
Renault	13	40	90
SAAB	17	40	93
Simca	4	34	88
Toyota	*	54	88
Volkswagen	26	67	93
Volvo	56	88	97

*The car make was not represented in Sweden at this time.

After about 16 years approximately one fourth (27 percent) of the originally registered passenger cars still remain, but there are great variations between the different makes. Thus the percentages remaining vary from below 4 percent up to 56 percent.

Table 7 table presents the median life for some major car makes in Sweden. Values calculated for 1965, 1971 and 1975–1978 are presented.

It can be seen in Table 7 that the median life varies considerably between different car makes. The car makes with the lowest values in 1978 were about three years below the average car and six to seven years below the highest value.

In Canada, road salt usage in many provinces has cut down considerably the median life expectancy of cars and trucks.

TABLE 7

MEDIAN LIFE FOR PASSENGER CARS OF CERTAIN CAR MAKES, CALCULATED FROM THE SCRAPPING FREQUENCIES FOR THE YEARS 1965, 1971 AND 1975–1978

Car make	Year					
	1965	1971	1975	1976	1977	1978
Average for all passenger cars	9.4	12.4	13.9	13.4	14.1	14.4
BMC	8.6	10.2	11.9	11.3	12.1	12.3
BMW	9.1	10.5	12.8	12.7	13.3	13.5
Citroën	7.8	10.2	12.5	12.7	13.9	13.8
DKW/Audi	8.3	9.9	11.9	11.6	12.0	12.4
Fiat	8.3	10.6	11.7	11.0	11.0	11.4
Ford	8.4	11.2	12.7	12.3	12.6	12.9
Mercedes-Benz	10.2	12.4	14.7	14.8	15.5	15.2
Opel	8.8	11.4	13.1	12.6	13.0	13.5
Peugeot	8.6	11.8	12.8	11.8	11.6	11.6
Renault	6.9	10.3	12.4	11.9	12.3	12.4
SAAB	9.0	11.6	12.2	12.0	12.5	13.1
Simca	7.3	9.9	11.6	11.1	11.2	12.2
Volkswagen	10.6	13.2	14.2	13.8	14.0	14.3
Volvo	10.7	14.2	16.5	16.7	17.5	17.9

SOURCE: *AB Svensk Bilprovning*, Sweden

Why Buyers Prefer Imports

American car manufacturers cannot understand why an increasing number of North American and European car buyers are thumbing their noses at American-built cars and choosing Japanese or European models instead. But, according to a February 1980 survey among 1200 Canadian car owners the answer is a simple one: better-quality cars.

Len Coates, a Canadian syndicated car columnist, asked motorists residing in Manitoba, Ontario, and Quebec to rate American and imported cars on reliability, quality control, fuel economy, and cold-starting performance.

More than two-thirds (68.7 percent) of import owners replied that they were happy with the reliability of their cars, while only one-half of the American-vehicle owners could say the same.

Chrysler products were invariably singled out for the "it's a lemon" designation, but, General Motors scored the most points for reliability, with Ford and American Motors falling in the middle range. Once again only 7 percent of the import car owners were "unhappy" with their vehicles.

Although most consumers don't take gas mileage claims seriously, fuel economy still represented another sore point among Mr. Coates' readers. American Motors had the most discontented owners in this group, with Ford and Chrysler close behind. GM and imported-car owners were relatively happy with their gas mileage.

Premature rusting and poor paint adhesion appears to be the nemesis of the American-car makers, according to the Coates survey. General Motors and Chrysler owners voiced the most dissatisfaction, while Ford did slightly better, possibly due to the "Rusty Ford" campaign of the mid-seventies. American Motors did better than the imports in this category, possibly because AMC has seldom had rust or paint problems while many of the imported cars had bodies that were practically biodegradable.

Cold-weather starting was the last category that gave General Motors, the imports, and Ford top marks. Those vehicles whose owners may still be trying to start them were American Motors and Chrysler.

It's obvious that new-car purchasers are influenced more by word-of-mouth reference than automotive advertising. And as long as the American car makers continue to produce poor-quality cars (particularly in the subcompact class), car buyers everywhere will choose an import instead.

Choosing the Right Size

Cars, like shoes, have to fit the customer who purchases them. Therefore, the size of a used car plays an important part in the potential satisfaction that car will give its owner. Some of the principal body sizes and their advantages and disadvantages are listed here.

Subcompacts.
Length: 150–175 inches
Wheelbase: 94–101 inches
Number of passengers: 4, but 2 in comfort
Mileage: 25–30 MPG
Safety: poor protection, may maximize injuries
Recommendation: an excellent urban car

Detroit was forced into the subcompact field as a result of the wide popularity of the imported subcompacts in the early 1960's. They offer excellent gas economy, easy maneuverability in urban areas, and have a low retail purchase price.

Most Japanese subcompacts are less safe than larger cars, though, and there is less room for passengers and baggage. Because of their small motors, shifting can be a problem with an automatic transmission and early motor failures are common with both Japanese and European subcompacts. Still, both Japanese and European subcompact models sell well due to their greater reliability and fuel economy when compared to American vehicles. Also, a greater use of the transverse engine has provided much more interior space.

One of the more alarming characteristics of subcompact highway performance is its vulnerability to lateral wind movements that may throw the car off course. Anyone who has driven a subcompact on a two-lane highway knows the gut fear experienced whenever a huge truck passes in the same lane or drives past in the opposite lane. Control can be difficult and sometimes impossible in these situations.

Compacts.
Length: 171–195 inches
Wheelbase: 102–108 inches
Number of passengers: 5, but 4 in comfort
Mileage: 20–25 MPG
Safety: very good
Recommendation: best car for city and highway driving

All of the American manufacturers admit that the future of the automobile industry rests with the compact car. This prognosis appears to be well founded since more North Americans buy compacts, both new and used, than any other size of automobile. Consumers are buying compact cars so they may benefit from the advantages of good gas mileage, adequate passenger space for five persons, better than average crash protection from collisions and a depreciation rate that is much lower than average. Typical compacts are the Valiant, Dart, Nova, Maverick and Hornet.

Compacts are also popular because they combine the advantages of a subcompact with the advantages of larger-sized cars. The trunk is usually large enough to accommodate the average baggage requirements and the interior space is more than adequate for the needs of the average family.

Intermediates.
Length: 196–203 inches
Wheelbase: 108–112 inches
Number of passengers: 6, but 5 in comfort
Mileage: 15–20 MPG
Safety: very good
Recommendation: good for highway driving but gas mileage low in city driving

The intermediates offer consumers an interior that can comfortably seat six while also providing more than enough space for luggage. High-speed performance is not spectacular, but does not require much effort on the driver's part to control the vehicle. Nevertheless, intermediates can still give from 10 to 15 miles to the gallon, and this is one plus that attracts a large clientele.

Intermediates are ill-suited for urban driving. Parking may be a problem and gas mileage suffers from the stop and go conditions of city traffic. Although as many as six persons may sit in this model there is no guarantee the seating will be comfortable for all six.

Safety is an advantage with this model. With its considerable weight and size, the intermediate-sized models provide more collision protection for passengers than the compacts. Of course, this added protection is costly because of increased fuel consumption.

Almost all the American automobile manufacturers are concentrating their present production on the compact and subcompact car models. Vehicles like the Oldsmobile are being built with engines which burn a leaner gas mixture and lighter weight body components made of plastic and metal alloys to conserve fuel.

Large cars.
Length: 204–217 inches
Wheelbase: 116 inches or more
Number of passengers: 6 in comfort
Mileage: 7–15 MPG
Safety: fair; recent tests show smaller cars absorb crash forces better
Recommendation: best car for extensive highway driving by motorists who can write off gasoline costs

The term "large car" is really relative. Generally, "large" is used to designate those vehicles having a wheelbase greater than 119 inches and weighing about 3500 pounds. Now that the car makers are shortening their large cars and cutting back on the excess poundage, pounds, wheelbase, and weight may no longer be an accurate indicator for designating a car's size. Most people consider vehicles in the Toronado, Continental, and Cadillac class as large cars, however.

Owners of large cars have to pay a considerable amount of money when buying or leasing their vehicles in addition to the higher insurance premiums that are usually charged. Despite this added cost, large-size cars offer an immeasurable amount of comfort at high speeds and incur minimal damage from front, rear, and side collisions. The Insurance Institute For Highway Safety confirms this fact with statistics that show the low claim payout associated with large used cars. Large cars depreciate slowly after their first four years of use and can often be bought at bargain prices. Since these models can also comfortably seat six adults, they make excellent second cars for families that like to take motoring vacations.

Choosing the Right Kind of Car
Four-door sedan. This is probably the most reliable used-car model available. There is usually plenty of rear-seat room, less road noise and body rattles, and a cheaper list price than other models. Also, the addition of side pillars increases the chances of surviving a rollover accident.

Two-door sedan. This model has all the advantages of the four-door sedan, except that the rear-seat passengers have less room to enter or leave the rear interior.

Four-door hardtop. Hardtops cost more than the other used-car models, and have a more streamlined appearance because of the absence of cause of the absence of side pillars. As a result, road noise and dirt enter into the interior more easily. This model is very popular because of its appearance, but chassis durability is not very great, with squeaks and rattles a common complaint.

Two-door hardtop. This model has essentially the same characteristics as the four-door hardtop but offers less back-seat space than other models. It is usually priced higher than the sedan.

Station wagons. If passenger and cargo space is a prime consideration, then a used station wagon is the answer. Station wagons still command high prices on the used-car market, though, so don't expect to pay less than $2000.

One of the most serious disadvantages of this model is the difficulty in keeping the interior heated in the winter. Exterior road noise is also a frequent problem because the interior has a tendency to echo normal road noise.

ACTIVE VS. PASSIVE AUTO SAFETY

Another factor that must be taken into consideration when purchasing a used car is the amount of safety the vehicle provides. In establishing guidelines for evaluating the relative safety of a used car the mechanical components of the vehicle must be examined to decide whether or not the car provides a sufficient degree of active and passive safety.

High-performance tires, improved braking systems, and specialized suspensions are typical elements that increase the degree of active safety available in a used car. Active safety components are generally only those mechanical components that help avoid accidents. Advocates of active safety stress that automobile accidents are caused by the proverbial "nut behind the wheel" and believe that safe driving can be taught through the public schools or by private driving schools.

The theory of active safety has several drawbacks. First, there is no independent proof that safe driving can be taught successfully. Even if a young driver learns how to master defensive driving techniques, there is still no assurance that this training will be of any use in an emergency situation where panic reflexes are most common.

TABLE 8
PERCENT OF ACCIDENT-INVOLVED VEHICLES
IN WHICH THE
MOST SERIOUS INJURY WAS FATAL OR SERIOUS

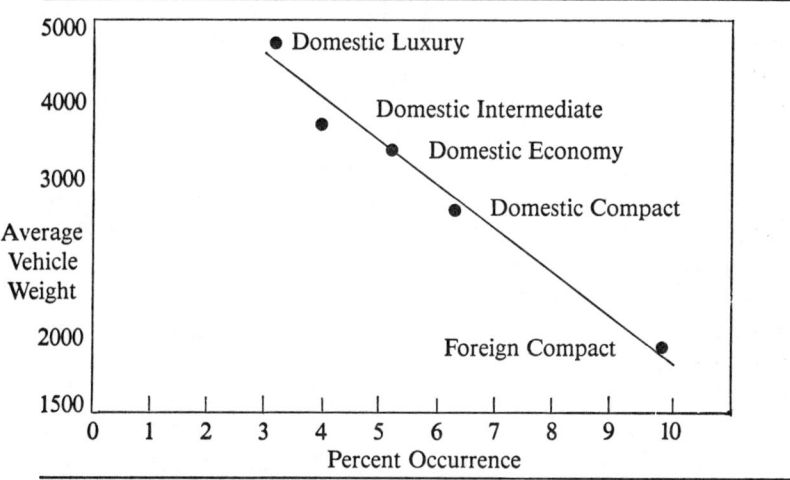

SOURCE: New York State Highway Department Study Conducted for Dot

Finally, it has been estimated that more than 50 percent of all fatal accidents are caused by drivers operating their vehicles while under the influence of alcohol or drugs. Surely all the high-performance options and specialized driving courses in the world will not provide much protection for such drivers or their victims.

Passive safety is a concept wherein the consumer accepts the fact that the car is going to be involved in an accident someday and when that accident occurs, the vehicle itself must provide as much protection as possible to the driver, the car's occupants, and other vehicles that may be struck. This collision protection must be provided without any dependence upon the driver's individual reaction. This, then, is passive protection.

Purchasing a used car with the idea that you will be involved in an accident is not an unreasonable assumption. According to the Insurance Institute for Highway Safety, the average car can be expected to have two accidents before being discarded. Doctor Robert Haddon, a spokesman for the IIHS, has testified before various United States congressional committee hearings in support of the concept of passive safety before, during, and after an automobile accident. In graphic detail, Haddon has shown films of 1975–1977 subcompact cars colliding with large vehicles and then careening out of control, exploding, or crumpling up to such an extent that the small-car occupants would be two and one-half times as likely to be killed as the occupants of a larger car. Advocates of passive safety do not intend to see every motorist driving around in cars similar to army tanks. In fact, recent crash tests have shown some small 1979 domestic subcompacts like the Chevette and Chrysler Omni/Horizon do very well in crashes of 35 MPH. The weight factor is mentioned, however, so that a potential used-car buyer will realize that the purchase of a small early production subcompact for high-speed driving along congested expressways adds an additional element of danger that he may not have considered.

Before leaving the question of vehicle weight as an element of safety, we have to also consider the loss of economy with heavier cars. Many car purchasers wonder just which car provides the best trade-off between fuel economy and safety. Under most driving conditions including both highway and city driving, many experts agree that a compact car of the Valiant or Nova category is the best compromise model.

Vehicle components may also affect the degree of passive protection an automobile can provide. Seatbelts, for example provide the best means of reducing the severity of injury arising from low-speed as well as high-speed frontal collisions. By preventing the ejection of the motorist and occupants from the vehicle, the National Safety Council estimates that a belted occupant has a five times greater chance of surviving an accident than an unbelted individual who prefers to be "thrown free." From a safety point of view, a used car without seatbelts should never be considered. Seatbelts can be installed for about $75.

Cars that have rear gas tanks that form the bottom of the rear trunk should also be shunned. This gas-tank design has already been the object of numerous lawsuits because the gas tank can split from a rear impact and spill gas and fumes throughout the rear trunk. The wiring of the rear tail lights can then ignite the fumes and turn the car into a mobile Molotov cocktail.

Finally, convertibles are not good risks when involved in automobile highway accidents. The roof design provides little protection for passengers should the car be involved in an accident that causes the vehicle to roll over. If you still insist upon purchasing a used convertible, have a roll bar installed for about $150.

The Small-Car Safety Myth

For years, both domestic and foreign car makers have had to contend with the myth that all small cars are deadly in high-speed accidents and, generally, most small import cars protect occupants better than small domestic vehicles.

These myths have been shattered by high-speed impact tests by the Washington-based National Highway Traffic Safety Administration, that showed many 1979 model domestic subcompact cars surpassed foreign models in crash protection as well as offered greater occupant protection than other larger domestic vehicles.

The NHTSA crashed 1979 model cars into a fixed barrier at 35 MPH and listed the following vehicles in order of their capacity to protect their occupants:

1. Chrysler Omni/Horizon
2. Ford Mustang
3. Chevrolet Chevette
4. Chevrolet Citation
5. Chrysler Cordoba
6. Buick Riviera

A number of other cars were found by the NHTSA to offer less protection to vehicle occupants than the vehicles listed above. Among them were the:

1. VW Rabbit
2. Datsun 210
3. Chrysler Champ/Colt (Mitsubishi)
4. Ford Pinto/Bobcat
5. Toyota Celica
6. GM Firebird/Camaro
7. Chrysler Volaré/Aspen
8. Ford Fairmont/Zephyr
9. Cutlass, Olds 98
10. Grand Prix
11. Impala
12. Electra
13. Catalina
14. Ford LTD
15. Mercury Marquis

16. Chrysler LeBaron/Diplomat
17. Chrysler St. Regis/Newport

Safety Standards

Since 1966, the federal government has forced automakers to provide safer new cars. Government regulations specify strict standards governing brakes, lights, tires, bumpers, side impact protection and hundreds of other mechanical components. The government has completed a preliminary report that covers the eight-year period that the American safety standards have been in effect. This report was submitted on July 21, 1976, by the United States General Accounting Office to the Senate Commerce Committee. It concluded that more than 30,000 lives had been saved by federal auto safety standards.

From the GAO report, it appears that certain model years provided more protection than others. For example, the report cites statistics that show that safety features reduced deaths and serious injuries by 15 to 25 percent on 1966-1968 model cars and cut deaths and injuries by 25 to 30 percent on 1969-1970 models when compared with pre-1966 models manufactured without the safety standards. Surprisingly, the report concluded that 1971-1973 model cars "showed little, if any, improvement."

American safety standards require the installation of equipment such as seatbelts, shoulder harnesses, improved windshield mountings, energy-absorbing steering columns, reinforced roofs and side doors and other special safety components. The government estimates that all this mandatory equipment has cost the manufacturers about $8.5 million, but, according to the GAO, the total cost of the devices "appears to be beneficial."

The American study underlines two important facts this used-car guide emphasizes: First, cars manufactured since 1975 have less quality and are quicker to deteriorate than pre-1975 models; and second, the use of passive protection measures as required by the federal government is far more effective in saving lives than voluntary measures that stress driver education.

Allstate's Best and Worst Cars

New and used cars from the 1977-1980 model years have been given 10 to 30 percent premium reductions due to their favorable "actual loss experience." Those cars benefiting from Allstate's premium reductions are:

1977 Models.
1. AMC Pacer and AMX
2. Buick Skylark
3. Chevrolet Malibu, Impala, Caprice and Nova
4. Chrysler Newport, New Yorker, Town and Country and Le Baron
5. Dodge Omni and Aspen
6. Mercury Marquis
7. Plymouth Horizon, Gran Fury and Volaré
8. Volvo

1978-1980 Models.
1. AMC Matador
2. Buick Century, Le Sabre, Estate Wagon, and Skylark
3. Chevrolet Impala, Caprice, Malibu, Nova and Citation
4. Chrysler Cordoba, Newport and Le Baron
5. Dodge Aspen, Diplomat, Mirada, Monaco, and St. Regis
6. Ford LTD
7. Mercury Marquis
8. Oldsmobile 88, Custom Cruiser, Toronado, and Omega
9. Pontiac Catalina, Phoenix, Bonneville, and Grand Safari
10. Plymouth Volaré
11. Toyota Cressida

Of course, Allstate also found a number of new and used vehicles that had an unfavorable reputation, and consequently adjusted premium costs upward. Those vehicles costing more to insure are:

1977 Models.
1. Buick Riviera
2. Chevrolet Camaro and Corvette
3. Dodge Colt
4. Ford Fiesta and Mustang
5. Lincoln Continental Mark IV and Mark V
6. Plymouth Arrow and Sapporo
7. Pontiac Firebird
8. Alfa Romeo
9. Audi
10. BMW
11. Datsun 210, 280Z, 200 SX and 810

12. Fiat
13. Jaguar
14. Lotus
15. Mazda RX 4
16. Mercedes-Benz
17. Peugeot
18. Toyota Corolla, Corona, Celica
19. VW Beetle, Rabbit, Scirocco and Porsche
20. Saab
21. Triumph TR7
22. Renault 17

1978–1980 Models.
1. Cadillac Eldorado
2. Chevrolet Camaro and Corvette
3. Dodge Challenger
4. Ford Mustang II
5. Lincoln Versailles, Continental, Mark V
6. Mercury Capri (1979 and 1980)
7. Oldsmobile Starfire
8. Plymouth Arrow and Sapporo
9. Pontiac Firebird
10. Alfa Romeo
11. Audi
12. BMW
13. Datsun B210, 200SX, and 280-Z
14. Fiat
15. Jaguar
16. Lancia
17. Lotus
18. Mazda GLC, Cosmo, RX3, RX7, and 626
19. MG
20. Opel
21. Porsche
22. Renault 5, 12, and 17
23. Saab
24. Subaru
25. Toyota Celica and Corolla
26. Triumph TR-7
27. VW Scirocco

Choosing a Safe Car

As previously mentioned, cars can be made unsafe by the way they are designed by the manufacturer. The smart used-car buyer can still eliminate many of the hazardous designs by carefully choosing the used-car model that offers the fewest dangers. Although no used car has been made without some designed-in dangers, there are some questionable designs and options that should definitely be avoided. The following list shows how manufacturers make an unsafe car:

1. Give a large expensive expanse of glass but neglect to give wipers large enough to clean a safe portion of the glass in hazardous conditions.
2. Place all lights at such low levels on the car body that they are easily damaged by minor accidents and easily obscured by road dirt and spray.
3. Put the headlights in cavelike recesses so at night, or when there is limited visibility, they cannot be seen from the side by other drivers. This will aid snow collection around the lights and force the car owner to pay for side running lights as well.
4. Complicate the headlight problem by installing concealing covers that are expensive to repair and can freeze closed in cold weather.
5. Put rear-view outside mirrors far enough away from the driver so that his field of vision is reduced, and no adjustment can be made from the driver's seat without expensive remote control options.
6. "Protect" the car with ornamental bumpers that only absorb 1 percent of the impact.
7. Give minimal or no protection to side-door panels, so that they are easily chipped when the door is opened or when another car touches them.
8. Construct "hidden" windshield wipers that get frozen into their cavelike compartments in winter, and get stuck up by leaves and other foreign matter in fall.
9. Construct "hidden" gas tanks that form part of the rear trunk compartment and may act as a "bomb" in rear-end collisions.
10. Provide woefully deficient heating-defrosting systems that reduce windshield visibility and drain battery reserve capacity to a dangerously low level.

MANUFACTURER'S RESPONSIBILITY FOR USED CARS

Even though a used car has been bought from a private seller and no longer falls within the limits of the normal new-car warranty given by the manufacturer, the manufacturer may still be held liable for damages cased by the vehicle's defective design. As mentioned before, the manufacturer is always liable for the replacement or repair of defective parts if independent testimony can show that the part was incorrectly manufactured or designed. Usually, the existence of a "secret" warranty extension will help prove the part had a high failure rate. In addition to replacing or repairing the part that failed, the automaker can also be held responsible for any consequential damages arising from the part's failure. In the past, this had meant that loss of wages, supplementary transportation costs, and damages for personal inconvenience could be awarded by the courts to owners of used cars.

Personal Injury Liability
Automobile dealers and manufacturers have been held responsible for injuries caused by used cars that had mechanical defects that *induced or caused* an accident.

Recent court decisions have begun to hold automobile manufacturers responsible for the *design* of their vehicles. In essence, the courts have decided that a manufacturer of a new or used motor vehicle is responsible for the injuries arising from an accident that were *aggravated* or *maximized* by faulty design. For example, even if an accident is *caused* by driver error and has nothing at all to do with a defective mechanical component, the manufacturer is responsible if injuries are caused by jagged protrusions in the passenger compartment, if fuel tanks exploded upon impact, or if any one of a thousand design features increased the severity of an injury in an automobile accident.

The desire of the American judiciary to make automobile manufacturers design their cars so that automobile accident injuries are minimized is of particular importance to used-car buyers who may be injured by poorly designed vehicles.

After-sale Servicing
A second area of manufacturer responsibility is servicing after purchase. The quality of this work varies, depending on dealer, and can be directly linked to the number of dealerships found within the dealer

network. Auto industry experts suggest that car makers with less than 700 dealers, throughout the United States, cannot guarantee an adequate supply of replacement parts and high-quality warranty servicing. Although this is not a problem with domestic car manufacturers (except for new models never presented before), a number of foreign-car makers are severely handicapped by a weak dealer network, as the following dealer breakdown shows:

TABLE 9

United States Foreign-Car Dealerships
(Up to January 30, 1980)

Japanese	**8817**	*Italian*	**1108**
Colt/Challenger	2225	Fiat	642
Arrow/Sapporo	2165	Alfa Romeo	234
Datsun	1079	Lancia	170
Toyota	1072	Ferrari	40
Mazda	773	Maserati	22
Subaru	753	*British*	**1090**
Honda	750	MG	358
Opel	0	Triumph	341
West German	**8030**	Jaguar	268
Fiesta	5482	Rolls-Royce	64
Volkswagen	1016	TVR	21
Audi	439	Lotus	20
Mercedes-Benz	410	Aston Martin	18
BMW	356	*French*	**1024**
Porsche	327	Renault	729
		Peugeot	295
		Swedish	**724**
		Volvo	408
		Saab	316
	TOTAL DEALERS	**20,793**	

For these reasons a manufacturer with a good reputation should be given preference in all situations.

PART TWO

Used Car Ratings

DEFINITION OF TERMS USED IN RATINGS

Gas Mileage

As a result of the increased cost of gasoline, motorists are justifiably concerned about gas mileages they can expect from various models. Unfortunately, mileage claims made by the major automobile manufacturers can be in error by as much as 20 percent. The gas-mileage figures cited in this guide are approximations based upon interviews with individual car owners. These figures may not be 100 percent correct either, since poor dealer servicing can screw up a car's mileage rating fairly drastically. Poor gas mileage can usually be corrected by a carburetion specialist, in most instances. A verification by such a specialist may cost as much as $25 just to diagnose the source of the problem. Nevertheless, corrective action can only be taken after this type of examination.

Taking off the factory-installed pollution-control devices may interfere with the normal operation of the motor and cause the premature wearing of the valves. Be wary of gas-saving "gadgets" that promise to reduce gasoline consumption by as much as 25 percent. More than a hundred such firms have been convicted of misleading advertising by the Federal Trade Commission.

Used cars that have not been abused or poorly serviced should give approximately the same gasoline mileage as indicated in the guide.

Selling Price

The selling price of any used car is determined by its popularity. Selling prices for used cars can also be affected by a host of other factors, such as: increased insurance rates, bad publicity surrounding a particular model (remember the Edsel?), and the reputation of the dealer body servicing that model.

Optional equipment rarely has a great influence upon the market value of a used car. In fact, some luxury options like electric seats and windows can be not only an embarrassment when they malfunction, but can also require costly repairs.

Used-car dealers will not agree with the prices listed in this guide. They will find the prices to be $500–$800 too low. This criticism is expected because used-car dealers often inflate the prices of their used cars this much to make a hefty profit on the sale and also cover the costs of any future warranty claims. The selling prices listed here eliminate the used-car dealer profit entirely.

The used-car prices given in this guide are for standard models in excellent condition equipped with a radio and automatic transmission. Calculate the current price by subtracting $50 for each month after May, 1981, for every car older than two years.

Premature Rusting and Paint Peeling

Auto-body specialists have helped prepare this guide's unique rusting and paint peeling diagrams that indicate which automobile models are most vulnerable to premature rusting. Specific body areas that may be particularly rust-prone are also shown. Not every model car is expected to follow the patterns in the rusting diagrams; however, areas that are noted to have little resistance to premature rusting should be examined very carefully by a specialist. Also, note that the diagrams are standardized so as to show more clearly rust-prone areas.

Recall Campaigns

Only a sample number of recall campaigns has been selected for each model car. Motorists can write the Department of Transportation in Washington, D.C. for a more complete list of vehicles recalled for safety-related defects since 1966. Just because a certain vehicle has been recalled a number of times does not mean that model represents a poor used-car buy. After all, even Rolls-Royce has had to recall a few of its models. The important thing to remember is to get that defect fixed.

Warranty Extensions

Most consumers are aware of the 12,000-mile warranty applied to new cars. However, automobile manufacturers also have a system of secret warranty extensions for vehicles that have defective components.

These warranty extensions often offer free parts and labor up to five years or 50,000 miles, regardless of the number of prior owners.

Many of the following "secret" warranty extensions are presently in force. Nevertheless, most manufacturers will deny that extended warranties exist. If this happens, write the Federal Trade Commission, Washington, D.C. 20580, for copies of internal company documents sent to the government.

Also, if the extended warranty's arbitrarily established time limit has elapsed, consumers may still demand that the dealer or manufacturer pay part of the repairs. Usually a small-claims-court lawsuit will bring quick results if all else fails.

What to Do?
Warranty Compensation Guidelines

Warranty extensions are made by manufacturers to compensate consumers for defective parts that either fail prematurely or never function properly from the start.

Lawyers advise consumers never to accept an automobile manufacturer's warranty limitation, whether it be for five years as with some Toyota and Vega/Astre warrantry extensions, or the normal 12,000-mile/12-month warranty. The lawyers feel that since the warranty extensions are for repairs caused by defective parts, dealers and car manufacturers cannot arbitrarily limit the extent of their liability. The law holds manufacturers responsible for their negligence regardless of what a dealer or factory representative may say to the contrary. Therefore, be wary of "goodwill" settlements where the dealer or manufacturer agrees to assume only 50 percent of the bill, or agrees to pay only for parts but not for the labor to install the parts. This type of "goodwill" is hard to accept, since the labor would not be necessary if the part was not defective.

Consumers wishing to contest a repair bill that may be excessive or covered by a secret warranty extension should take the following steps:

1. Write a registered letter to dealer and car manufacturer asking that repairs be covered by the warranty or by an extended warranty.

2. If the request is refused, pay for repairs and then make a claim for reimbursement through the small-claims court.

3. Be sure to send a subpoena to the manufacturer ordering the deposit of all internal documents relating to the warranty extension for that model car. Refer to documents published in this book.

Consumer groups keep on file a list of small-claims-court cases where consumers have forced manufacturers to extend their warranties for cars well after the normal warranty has expired. Some court judgments have extended the warranty far beyond the normal warranty period.

Auto Emissions Warranty

According to federal law, *if...*
- Your car is less than 5 years old and has less than 50,000 miles; and
- An original engine part fails because of a defect in materials or workmanship; and
- The part failure causes your car to exceed federal emissions standards; *then...*

the car manufacturer must repair or replace the defective part free of charge. This is the protection given car owners under the Emissions Design and Defect Warranty required by the Clean Air Act.

The emissions warranty applies to all motor vehicles manufactured since 1972, including cars, pickups, recreational vehicles, heavy-duty trucks, and motorcycles. However, the length of your warranty coverage, as expressed by a time or mileage limitation called "useful life," is different for each type of vehicle. For example, the warranty or useful life for cars is 5 years or 50,000 miles, whichever occurs first. To determine the length of warranty coverage that applies to your vehicle, look for the emissions warranty description in your owner's manual or warranty booklet.

Beginning with cars manufactured in the 1972 model year you will find an explanation of the emissions warranty in your owner's manual, or warranty booklet.

Under the law, each manufacturer must honor the warranty if the three conditions listed above occur.

The emissions warranty applies to used cars. Yes. It does not matter if you bought your car new or used, from a dealer or anyone else. As long as your vehicle has not exceeded the warranty time or mileage limitations, this warranty applies.

Parts and repairs are covered by the emissions warranty. Coverage includes: (1) any part whose primary purpose is to control emissions, and (2) any part that has an effect on emissions.

To aid in identifying specific parts in your car, the two categories are listed (Tables 10 and 11). They are further divided into systems, with a list of the major parts in each system.

Emissions-control parts. These are parts which the manufacturer has included in the car to control emissions. If one of these parts fails because of a defect in materials or workmanship, it will probably cause your car's emissions to exceed federal standards. Therefore, these parts, if defective, should be repaired or replaced under the emissions warranty:

TABLE 10
Emissions-Control Parts

Exhaust Gas Recirculation (EGR) System
- EGR Valve
- EGR Spacer Plate
- Thermal Vacuum Switch
- EGR Backpressure Transducer

Evaporative Emissions Control System
- Evaporative Canister

Crankcase Emissions Control System
- PCV Valve

Early Fuel Evaporative (EFE)/Heat Riser Systems
- EFE Valve
- Thermal Vacuum Switch
- Heat Riser Valve

Air Injection System
- Air Pump
- Anti-Backfire (Diverter Valve)
- Reed Valve

Catalytic and Exhaust Gas Conversion Systems
- Catalytic Converter
- Thermal Reactor
- Oxygen Sensor

Spark Advance Control System
- Vacuum Advance Unit
- Transmission Controlled Spark Switches
- Electronic Spark Controls

Hoses, gaskets, brackets, clamps, and other accessories used in the above systems.

Emissions-related parts. There are other parts of your car which have a primary purpose other than emissions control, but which nevertheless have significant effects on your car's emissions. If any of these parts fail to function, your car's emissions may exceed federal standards. Therefore, when any of the parts of the following systems are defective in materials or workmanship and have failed in a way that would be likely to cause your car's emissions to exceed federal standards, they should be repaired or replaced under the emissions warranty:

TABLE 11
Emissions-Related Parts

Carburetion System	
• Carburetor	• Choke
Fuel Injection System	
• Fuel Injectors	• Fuel Distributor
Air Induction System	
• Thermostatically Controlled Air Cleaner	• Air Box
Ignition System	
• Distributor	• Spark Plugs
• Electronic Controls	• Ignition Wires and Coil
Hoses, gaskets, brackets, clamps, and other accessories used in the above systems.	

If the manufacturer will not honor a valid emissions warranty claim. If your car has a defect in any of the components listed previously, you should contact an authorized warranty representative and follow the procedures outlined earlier. If that person denies your warranty claim, contact the person designated by the manufacturer for further warranty assistance.

You are entitled to pursue any independent legal actions you consider appropriate to obtain coverage under the emissions warranty. In addition, the Environmental Protection Agency is authorized to investigate the failure of manufacturers to comply with the terms of this warranty. If you have followed your manufacturer's procedures for making a warranty claim as set out in your owner's manual or warranty booklet and you are not satisfied with the manufacturer's determination, you are encouraged to contact EPA by writing:

In summary.
If a part in a listed system is defective:
• Present a warranty claim to an authorized warranty representative.

If your warranty claim is denied:
- Ask for the reason for the denial, in writing.
- Follow the appeal procedures in your owner's manual.

Recommended and Nonrecommended Models

Models are evaluated according to the total impression they give. Some of the factors contributing to this evaluation are: availability and cost of parts, warranty performance on the part of the manufacturer, dealership servicing, rate of depreciation, corrosion protection, and prior model performance.

Some models rated as "not recommended" may become acceptable used-car buys if an independent mechanic finds few major defects and if the buyer is willing to accept certain disadvantages such as parts shortages, poor dealer servicing, and a rapid rate of depreciation. On the other hand, some models that are rated as "recommended" may actually be unacceptable because they have been poorly maintained by previous owners. No car, however, should be dismissed as a "lemon" unless an independent mechanic's examination confirms the fact.

Used-Car Bargains

Used-car buyers who care little about the color or appearance of their car can often find real bargains in cars that have unpopular colors or have little or no optional equipment. European cars that have an incredibly fast rate of depreciation (Fiat and Renault, for example) can also be purchased for next to nothing. Most of the used-car bargains fall somewhere within the following categories:

The orphans. These cars are cheap because the manufacturer no longer makes that particular model. Yet, the vehicle may have been very popular and a reliable means of transportation. Some of the cars that fall into this category are the Ford Falcon, American Motors Javelin and Ambassador, the Dodge Colt, and the Chrysler Valiant and Dart. When shopping for orphaned used cars, be sure to select a model that was fairly popular so that an adequate supply of used parts can be found.

The uglies. These cars are distinguished by their lack of esthetic appeal to many motorists. Models such as the Gremlin and possibly the Hornet could fall into this classification. Don't judge ugly cars too harshly. Remember, beauty is only skin (sheet metal?) deep!

THE 1979 AND 1980 MODELS

During the 1979 and 1980 model year runs, most automobile manufacturers continued the trend of building more compact versions of their traditionally large cars or building larger versions of their small, compact cars and boosting sales prices by loading their small cars with options that once sold as standard equipment. Needless to say, there were very few mechanical innovations and what changes there were consisted in the restyling of exterior appearance and reworking the sheet metal so that a Valiant could be called a Volaré, or a Cricket/Colt could be transformed into an Arrow selling for a few hundred dollars more.

Some new models were introduced in 1979–1980, but public reaction was generally profoundly apathetic and such models as the Chevy front-wheel-drive Citation and the AMC Eagle were greeted by a lackluster public response. Although it is still too early to be precise about all models, one can still be safe in assuming that they continued the current North American trend in putting out bland cars.

Pricing the 1979 and 1980 Models

The new-car selling prices of these models at the retail level has been raised approximately 8 percent for each succeeding model year. This new-car price increase translates into about $500 for each new model. For used cars, and this includes cars advertised as "executive-driven," "mint condition," and "used demonstrator," the astute buyer will still deduct 30 percent from the new-car selling price for used cars that are one year old and another 20 percent for any 1980 model selling as a used car in September, 1981, because the car would then be two years old and worth only 50 percent of its initial new-car retail selling price.

Of course, there are exceptions to this rule of 50 percent depreciation during the first two years; however, these exceptions generally involve classic cars, like the 1965 Mustang; recreational vehicles, like the Jeep series; and high-performance sports cars, like the Corvette and Mercedes-Benz Coupe. In fact, the value of these vehicles continues to be artificially inflated by the public to such an extent that "black market" used-car prices for these cars are expected to continue with the 1981 model-year series.

Another group of cars that has so far escaped the "grim reaper" of depreciation is the quality foreign used car, such as vehicles manufacture by BMW, Mercedes-Benz, and Alfa Romeo, who continue to find a solid new- and used-car market despite the high price of their models.

An investment in one of these high-priced models is seldom a losing proposition (unless one buys a used Porsche with a cracked engine block).

Used-Car Availability

The year 1979–1980 was a bust for most auto manufacturers. As a result, General Motors, Ford, and Chrysler should have an oversupply of used, privately leased, and rental cars on the used-car market in the summer of 1981. These vehicles should carry the normal 30 percent depreciation value and have an ample supply of parts because of their popularity.

For those vehicles that had a bad selling year in 1980, their status will not change much once they get on to the used-car market. It is expected that present new-car buying trends will continue to such an extent that the only new-car manufacturers that should regain new-car sales are American Motors and General Motors. An investment in a used American Motors product (except the potentially rust-prone Pacer) is likely to be a good long-term used-car buy.

Another big loser in the 1981 new-car selling year, the Ford Motor Company, saw its number-two spot in new-car sales challenged by the Japanese. Because of Ford's bland model lineup, it is not likely that 1981 models will do any better. Consumers are, therefore, advised to steer away from most Ford used-car offerings. Incidentally, Ford used cars are expected to have a greater-than-average used-car depreciation rate. Ford's 1980 models should be depreciated an average of 35 percent of their original suggested manufacturers' retail price.

American Models

GENERAL MOTORS SUBCOMPACTS

Being General Motors means not having to say you're sorry—except on rare occasions like the bugging of Ralph Nader or the building of the Vega. For some strange reason GM just can't get its act together when manufacturing subcompact cars. All of its subcompact line reads like a disaster movie, with the new "international car," the Chevette, leading the way. Fortunately for GM and the rest of the country, as General Motors executives are wont to say, what sales have been lost in the subcompact lines have been more than made up by a resurgence of compact and intermediate sales. It seems the North American public is keenly aware that GM makes the best cars on the market except for subcompacts and luxury models.

Most 1977–1980 large cars and intermediates have been trimmed about 800 pounds and are approximately 12 inches shorter.

Vega

Panicked by the enthusiasm with which North Americans were describing and purchasing imported subcompacts in 1970, General Motors rushed into production its own subcompact, calling it "The tough little fun car" in an unprecedented media blitz.

Well, the car itself was unprecedented, except, of course, for the hazardous Corvair, as many new-Vega buyers would soon learn. Vegas began to have a reputation for oil-burning and defective motors that forced GM to extend the warranty. Next, the fenders started rusting away, especially in regions where corrosion is a problem, like Florida, New England, California, and Texas. So the warranty was extended for free fenders and motors to all owners of new and used Vegas. Other production problems which caused defective automatic transmissions led to the demise of the Vega. It should be noted in passing, however, that GM also extended the warranty for five years or 50,000 miles to cover this problem, too.

The Vega was a bad car. From 1971–1974 Vega owners reported that their vehicles were constantly breaking down or being taken back to the dealership for the correction of numerous safety defects. Now owners can't even pawn off their cars because the legend of the Vega has spread.

Parts availability for Vegas is good since there are quite a few already stocked in junk yards. Depreciation is so fast that GM dealers are embarrassed when owners come by to trade in their Vega. The Vega's chief used-car clientele seems to be young first-time car buyers looking for cheap transportation. General Motors improved the 1975–1977 models somewhat, but *no* Vega is recommended for any model year, unless you have a burning desire to learn mechanics *quick*.

Technical Specifications

Two-door model:	1975	1976	1977
Wheelbase	97"	97"	97"
Length	175"	175"	175"

Two-door model:	1975	1976	1977
Width	65"	65"	65"
Weight	2500 lb.	2500 lb.	2500 lb.
Standard motor	4 cyl.	4 cyl.	4 cyl.
Gas mileage	26.4	27.1	26.3
Price*	$1000	$1300	$1500

Not recommended: 1971–1974, and use caution when contemplating the purchase of post-1974 models.

---

*The used-car prices given are for standard models in excellent condition, equipped with a radio and automatic transmission. Calculate the current price by subtracting $50 for each month after May, 1981, for every car older than two years.

Chevette

General Motors launched the Chevette on the market in late 1976. Calling the new subcompact its "international car," GM priced the car to sell as the cheapest domestic subcompact available. This sales strategy was so successful that General Motors still outsells all its domestic rivals in the subcompact-car class because of the Chevette's low price, attractive styling and two- and four-door versatility.

But the car has more than its share of mechanical and body deficiencies. Beset by mechanical defects affecting the motor, brakes and transmission (the infamous 200-series), the Chevette is not recommended at any price. Its body problems include premature rusting, water leaks, and excessive paint peeling. Depreciation is rapid; parts are priced moderately but they are not easily obtained.

Although 1976–1977 models had serious safety-related defects, the 1979 and 1980 models were considerably improved. The car also has passed the federal government's 35 MPH crash tests where many Japanese and European models were eliminated.

Technical Specifications

Two-door model:	1977	1978	1979	1980
Wheelbase	94"	94"	94"	94"
Length	160"	160"	160"	162"
Width	62"	62"	62"	62"
Weight	2000 lb.	2000 lb.	2000 lb.	2000 lb.
Standard motor	6 cyl.	6 cyl.	6 cyl.	6 cyl.
Gas mileage	30	30	30	31

Two-door model:	1977	1978	1979	1980
Price	$2400	$2900	$3500	$4200

Not recommended

Rusting Diagrams for Vega and Chevette

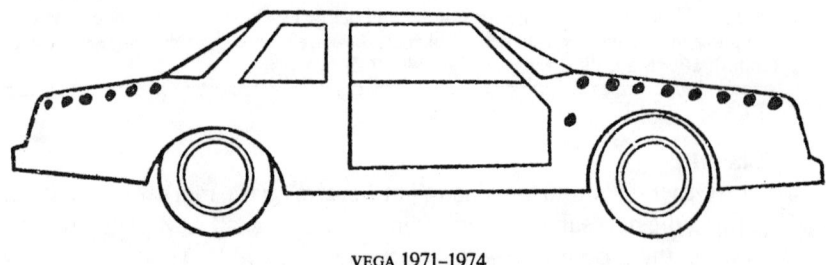

VEGA 1971–1974

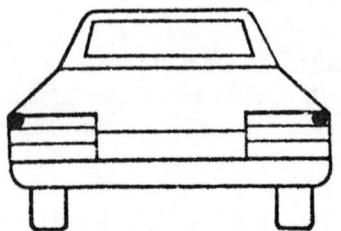 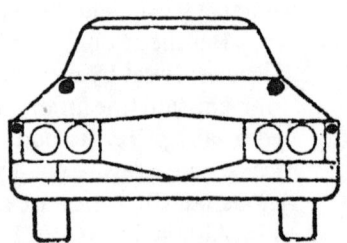

VEGA 1975–1977

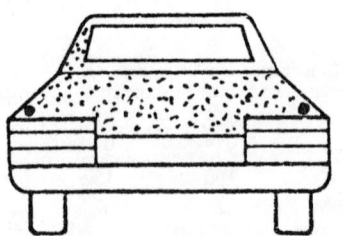 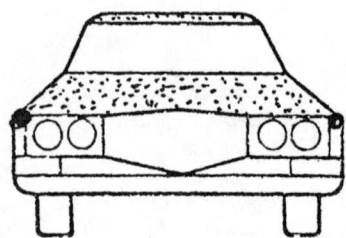

CHEVETTE 1977–1979

Defect Register

Affected Model	Defect
1976 Chevrolet Chevette	The seal between the fuel-tank filler neck and the fuel-tank filler cap may be inadequate and may leak fuel in a rollover.
1976 Chevette	These vehicles may experience, over rough terrain, a fatigue failure of the right brake pipe at the connection.
1976 Chevrolet models Vega and Monza 2+2; Pontiac models Astre and Sunbird equipped with the L-4 engine and two-barrel carburetor	Vehicles were assembled with an incorrect carburetor.
1976 Chevette	During certain driving conditions, it is possible for one or both of the front brake hoses to become hooked on the rear end of the upper control arm cross shaft of the front wheel suspension.
1976 and 1977 Chevette	Possibility that these vehicles' fuel systems may not comply with requirement of Federal Motor Vehicle Safety Standard No. 301, "Fuel System Integrity."

FORD SUBCOMPACTS

Ford rushed several subcompact cars brought over from England into production in the United States in 1970 to counter the foreign subcompact invasion. Most of these models were dismal failures, although none failed as badly as General Motors' model lineup. Because Ford's share of the domestic new-car market has hovered around 20-25 percent, its subcompact failures were particularly painful. Unfortunately for Ford, its other model lines were not as strong as General Motors', therefore the sales slack could not be taken up by the merchandising of other popular models as GM had done.

The quality of all Ford's models from the luxury to the subcompact cars also suffered from poor quality control. The most serious manifestation of this lack of quality began to show up in early 1972 when Ford discovered that its cars would rust *from one to two years earlier than the competition.* Of course, this was a major problem of tremendous consequence since Ford knew very well that the North American consumer might accept rusty fenders or a defective motor, but it was certain that the public would be up in arms against Ford if it were to find out that new Fords would have rust perforations all over the car before five years had passed. In regions where annual automobile safety inspections were mandatory, Ford knew that its vehicles had a good chance of being rejected by transport authorities. So, Ford decided secretly to extend its warranty coverage against rust.

Unfortunately, Ford's "J-67" secret warranty extension for the premature rusting of its 1971–1975 cars was denied to many Ford owners who were originally supposed to receive compensation. Now, as Ford had predicted, owners are angry over Ford's refusal to give owners of rust-cankered vehicles adequate indemnity. In Miami, Florida's Consumer Advocate for Dade County, Walter Dartland, has received more than 2500 complaints from irate owners of 1969–1974 rusted-out Fords. Several United States class actions have been settled out of court. Transport officials have discovered that full-sized 1965–1973 Ford models may have catastrophic failures of the idler arm assembly because of excessive corrosion. Should this failure occur, steering would become impossible.

Presently, the purchase of any used 1971–1975 Ford model is very risky. Even some of the most reliable models like the Comet and Maverick should be carefully inspected for rust damage before purchase. Most Fords depreciate rapidly because of their reputation for premature rusting and excessive gas consumption.

Pinto/Bobcat

The Pinto was launched in 1971 by Ford in an effort to compete with foreign imports and other domestic subcompacts. The car was initially well received (like the Vega); however, Ford soon discovered its Pinto had major motor, transmission (C-4), carburetor, and paint defects in addition to a serious premature corrosion problem. Sales soon started shifting to Ford's larger models.

The Pinto has a good braking system, excellent manual transmission, and almost adequate steering components. As with the Vega, the car has remained virtually unchanged since its first introduction. This is too bad because the Pinto has some serious mechanical shortcomings. For example, the suspension system makes high-speed handling extremely difficult and passenger space is both inadequate and poorly designed. Since 1974, the Pinto has been plagued with poor gas economy. This same problem has also affected the Pinto's twin, the Bobcat, sold by Mercury dealers.

Two of the most serious mechanical defects affecting Pinto/Bobcat models are the premature failure of the pistons in the motor (euphemistically referred to by Ford as "piston scuffing" and covered by an extended warranty) and the failure of the lip seal on the high clutch pack of C-3 automatic transmissions. There are no service bulletins from Ford about this problem; however, the easiest correction to make is to install a General Motors 350 seal in the affected transmissions.

Pinto/Bobcat models manufactured between 1971 and 1976 also have poorly designed gas tanks that can easily rupture from rear-end collisions. More than 1.5 million vehicles were recalled, but it is estimated that no more than 70 percent of the affected units were finally fixed. Used-car purchasers have the right to the free repair.

Parts availability should be no problem for Pinto/Bobcat owners. It's not surprising that both the Pinto and Bobcat have rapid rates of depreciation and are difficult to sell on the used-car market.

Pintos and Bobcats are barely a step above GM's Vega, which is another way of saying that a bicycle may be a safer and much more reliable means of transportation.

Technical Specifications

Two-door model:	1976	1977	1978	1979	1980	1975
Wheelbase	94"	94"	94"	94"	94"	94"
Length	169"	169"	169"	169"	170"	169"
Width	69"	69"	69"	69"	69"	69"
Weight	2500 lb.	2400 lb.	2400 lb.	2500 lb.	2400 lb.	2500 lb.
Standard motor	4 cyl.	4 cyl.	4 cyl.	4 cyl.	4 cyl.	4 cyl.
Gas mileage	26	26	20	26	26	18
Price	$1700	$2000	$2500	$3000	$3700	$1300

Not recommended

Rusting Diagrams for Ford Pinto/Bobcat, Maverick/Comet, Mustang, Fairlane, Falcon, Galaxie, Cougar

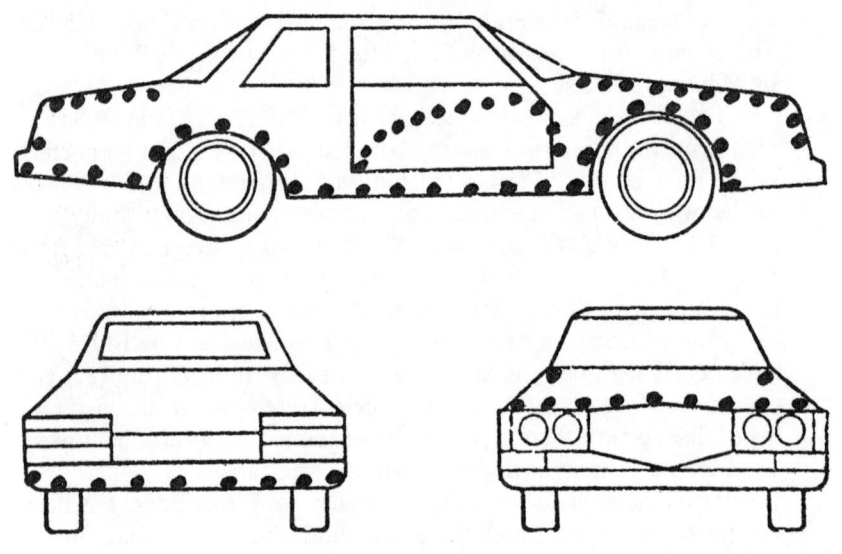

1971–1976

Rusting Diagram for Ford Custom/Galaxie

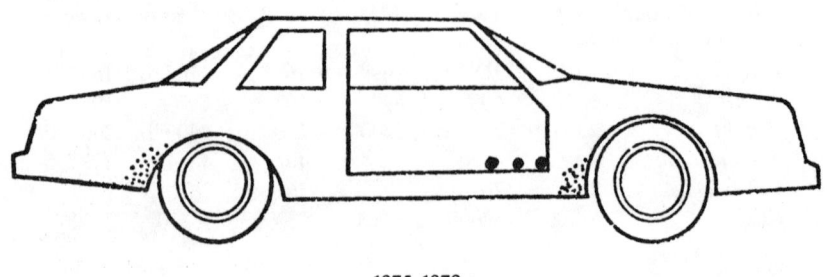

1975–1978

Defect Register

Affected Model	*Defect*
1971–1976 Ford Pinto and 1975–1976 Mercury Bobcat	Possibility that fuel tanks and filler neck installed on these vehicles are subject to failure when vehicles are struck from rear.
1976 Ford Pinto and Mustang, Mercury Bobcat	Possibility that vehicle may fail to meet requirements of 30 mph frontal barrier impact test.
1976 Ford Pinto passenger vehicles built from June 15 to June 30, 1976	Rear-seat cushion assembly cushion-to-underbody attaching brackets may separate from the seat frame as a result of inadequate spot welds; seats do not comply with federal law.
1976 Ford Pinto and Mustang and Mercury Bobcat vehicles built between May 28, 1976 and June 8, 1976	The screws that secure the latch striker to the seat-cushion frame were improperly processed and are subject to hydrogen embrittlement fracturing so that the latch will not meet the requirements of federal law.
1977 Ford Pinto and Mustang Mercury Bobcat vehicles equipped with 2.3-liter engines and Holley model	The power valve restrictor cross-drilling plug installed at the base of the carburetor fuel bowl may loosen or dislodge, causing accumulation of under-hood fuel vapors.
1976 Pinto, Bobcat, Maverick, Comet, Granada, Monarch, Torino, Elite, Montego, Cougar, Ford, Mercury, Thunderbird, Lincoln and Mark IV passenger vehicles and Ranchero trucks manufactured between December 1, 1975 and March 24, 1976	Certain 1976-model Ford and Lincoln-Mercury vehicles are equipped with accelerator cables that incorporate a stamped fitting at the dash-panel attachment location. The suspect cable assemblies contain fittings in which the bushing shoulder retaining bead is oversized, which may cause the bushing to dislodge during full acceleration. A dislodged bushing could hold the carburetor at a half-open throttle position.
1976 Ford Pinto and Mustang II and Mercury Bobcat vehicles equipped with 2.3-liter engines	The 2.3-liter engine in the affected vehicles may experience fuel leakage at the rubber hose connecting the fuel tube to the carburetor fuel filter. Fuel leakage would be accompanied by fuel odors and the possibility of an under-hood fire.

Affected Model	Defect
1978 Ford Pinto and Mustang, Mercury Bobcat	Possibility that automatic locking rear seat belt may fail to lock.
1977 Ford Maverick and Mercury Comet	The left front door-lock assemblies may be defective so that the left front door could open while the vehicle is in motion.
1976 Model Maverick, Comet, Torino, Elite and Montego vehicles equipped with air conditioning	Shifting of the heater-defroster system selector control from certain heating, ventilation and air-conditioning modes to the defrost mode may result in a delay in movement of the mode door.
1977 Ford Maverick and Mercury Comet equipped with 200, 250 and 302 CID engines and automatic transmissions	Some of the affected vehicles were produced with incorrect speedometer gears resulting in lower-than-actual speedometer and odometer readings.
1978 Ford Mustang II vehicles equipped with 2.8-liter engines	The dust tube portion of the accelerator cable assembly was improperly crimped so that the spring guide tube may bind when the accelerator is fully depressed. This condition could reduce the throttle return rate or prevent the full closure of the throttle plate when the accelerator is released.
1976 Mustang II vehicles equipped with power steering and manufactured on March 10 and March 11, 1976	Suspect units may contain a cracked or sheared valve sleeve drive pin in the steering gear pinion assembly.

Fiesta

Ford first brought its Fiesta to the United States from Europe in late 1977 to fill in the gaps in its model lineup between the Pinto/Bobcat, dropped in 1981, and the new Escort/Lynx. Now, with the Escort/Lynx selling well, it is the Fiesta's turn to be phased out.

The 1978 Fiesta, although originally priced around $4000, never did sell very well, because of the more attractive styling of the Japanese and other European imports. Still, depreciation has been average, with the Fiesta's fuel economy reaching 30 MPG.

Most of the Fiesta's problems are caused by inadequate dealer servicing and parts distribution. Replacement parts are also priced unrealistically high.

Mechanical problems concern chiefly the motor and front brakes. Ford has extended the warranty on new and used Fiestas with brake defects. The company pledges to pay for brake repairs to the brake disc and rotors if the vehicle has not exceeded two years or 24,000 miles.

Now that the Fiesta is to be taken off the market, its acute parts shortage is certain to become chronic.

Technical Specifications

Two-door model:	1978	1979	1980
Wheelbase	89"	89"	89"
Length	147"	147"	147"
Width	62"	62"	62"
Weight	1800 lb.	1800 lb.	1700 lb.
Standard motor	6 cyl.	6 cyl.	6 cyl.
Gas mileage	30	36	35
Price	$2900	$3600	$4100

Not recommended

Rusting Diagram for Ford Fiesta

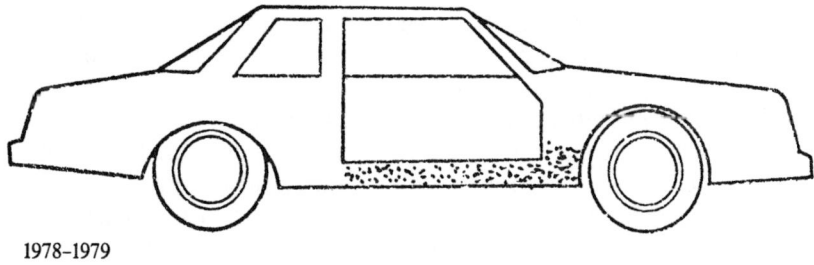

1978-1979

Defect Register

Affected Model	*Defect*
1978 Ford Fiesta vehicles equipped with dealer-installed air conditioning	Some air-conditioning kits may contain improperly located blower-motor resistor wires which could contact the polypropylene blower housing. Should the blower motor become jammed, sufficient heat may develop in the resistor wire to ignite the blower housing, causing a vehicle fire.
1978 Ford Fiesta	Incorrect information shown on placard provided to meet S4.3 of Federal Motor Vehicle Safety No. 110.
	Possibility vehicles were equipped with 4.50 × 12 inch steel wheels which may have mislocated valve stem holes.

Capri

Ford's best European car. After all, with the Cortina disaster, Ford of Europe had to make some move to bolster its European import reputation in the United States.

The Capri is one Ford car that has remained popular, despite parts problems and the difficulties involved in finding mechanics capable of servicing the Capri competently. Unfortunately, the early 1971 and 1972 Capri models suffered from the incurable rusting disease and dealer neglect that have run other good Ford cars into the ground. In addition, interior space in these early Capri models was inadequate, and quality-control defects abounded, including problems with the front disc brakes, windshield wipers, heater, defroster, alternator, and regulator. Many early Capris also had trouble with excessive shimmy in the front suspension, high oil consumption, hood-cable breakage, and door-adjustment problems. Ford has made secret warranty extensions for many of these defects, but actually receiving compensation may be difficult.

Anyone wishing to purchase a used Capri would be wise to buy a post-1973 model made in Germany. Of these models, the 1975 Capri 2 is the best used-car buy, with the 1974 six-cylinder Capri placing second. In overall driving performance, Ford's European Capri makes the American-built Ford Mustang II look like the old gray mare.

The 1979 and 1980 Capri models were built in America, and they are not as peppy or as comfortable as the earlier cars. Still, a relatively low retail price and good parts availability make these models excellent used-car buys.

Technical Specifications

Two-door model:	1976	1977	1978	1979	1980
Wheelbase	96"	96"	100"	100"	100"
Length	175"	175"	175"	179"	179"
Width	69"	70"	70"	69"	69"
Weight	2800 lb.	3000 lb.	2700 lb.	2500 lb.	2600 lb.
Standard motor	6 cyl.	6 cyl.	6 cyl.	6 cyl.	6 cyl.
Gas mileage	22	22	22	24	23
Price	$1900	$2600	$3300	$4000	$5000

Not recommended except in 1977 and 1978

Rusting Diagram for Capri

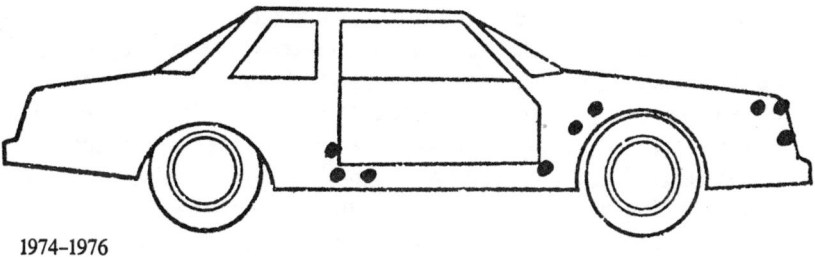

1974–1976

Defect Register

Affected Model	Defect
1973 Capri	Possibility of gasoline or gas-fumes leakage.
1974 Capri (2.8 mtr.)	Possibility of defective brake lines or master cylinder.
1974 and 1976 Capri 1 and Capri 2 (manufactured in Germany)	Front brake system may be defective.
1979 Mercury Capri and Ford Mustang	Possibility that vehicles may have been produced with incorrect steering gear coupling flanges which could slip on ratchet on steering gear input shaft and thereby cause reduction or loss of steering control.

CHRYSLER SUBCOMPACTS

Traditionally, Chrysler has stressed engineering over styling, but, during the past few decades Chrysler has begun to sacrifice engineering quality for popular styling innovations.

The best car models manufactured by Chrysler were always the subcompact and compact car lines. Vehicles such as the Valiant, Dart, and Colt/Arrow continued to run away with Chrysler sales. On the other hand, the highly publicized Cordoba model that mimics GM's successful Monte Carlo has done little to get Chrysler back on its feet.

Colt/Arrow

Actually, the Dodge Colt is a Japanese car. Through a special agreement with Mitsubishi, Chrysler has succeeded in obtaining the rights to mass-produce its own subcompact cars in Japan and service the same cars through its dealer network in the United States. The result has been a high-quality car that has not lacked parts, service, or demand in the North American new- and used-car markets.

Originally, Chrysler attempted to build its Colt and Cricket models in England. After realizing how difficult it would be to control the quality of its subcompacts imported from Britain, Chrysler decided to stick with the Japanese. The decision was a farsighted one because, just three years later, the Colt and Arrow models had a combined total sales record of almost 25,000 sales for the first five months of 1976.

Consumers find that the Colt/Arrow is easy to repair at any Chrysler dealer. Depreciation is less rapid than with other models and tradein demand is relatively high. Fuel economy is excellent while periodic maintenance is minimal. Even though Chrysler would like to take credit for the quality found in this model, the real credit must be given to the Mitsubishi Corporation which built these models under contract to Chrysler. If the job had been left to Chrysler, who knows what monstrous hybrid would have been spawned.

Some Colts were sold under the Cricket label because they were manufactured by Chrysler of England. These cars are misfits and do not incorporate the same engineering quality found with the Japanese Colt/Arrow. These English models also were recalled for some defective steering components discovered by the Department of Transportation.

Colts and Arrows should make excellent used-car buys. The only recurring mechanical defects concern the premature wearing of the disc brakes, the rusting-out of the front fenders, exploding oil filters and defective engine balancer (latter two problems covered by an extended warranty). Apart from these defects, the Colt/Arrow should be an excellent buy.

Technical Specifications

Two-door model:	1975	1976	1977	1978	1979	1980
Wheelbase	95"	95"	95"	92"	92"	92"
Length	172"	172"	172"	163"	163"	163"
Width	61"	61"	61"	61"	61"	61"
Weight	2250 lb.	2200 lb.	2100 lb.	2100 lb.	2100 lb.	2100 lb.
Standard motor	4 cyl.	4 cyl.	4 cyl.	4 cyl.	4 cyl.	4 cyl.
Gas mileage	25	26	27	28	28	29
Price	$1200	$1700	$2200	$2700	$3100	$4100

Recommended

Rusting Diagrams for Chrysler Colt/Arrow

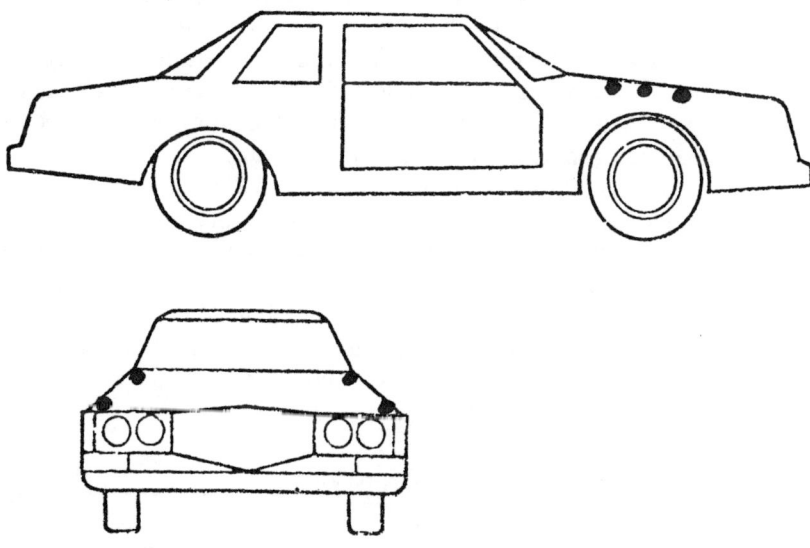

1975–1980

Defect Register

Affected Model	*Defect*
1977 Plymouth Arrow and Dodge Colt vehicles	The front hydraulic brake-hose assemblies have failed flexing requirements of federal law. This condition can cause a loss of brake fluid and a reduction of front-braking effectiveness.
1976 Plymouth Arrow and Dodge Colt vehicles equipped with a 1600-c.c. engine and automatic transmission	Driveline vibration dampers are subject to failure so that the detached portion of the damper could create a hazard to other vehicles should it land on the roadway.
1978 Dodge Colt, Challenger and Plymouth Arrow, Sapporo	Possibility of engine compartment fuel leakage due to inadequate staking operation allowing fuel to leak by fuel pump diaphragm and discharge out of pump body through breather hole.

Omni/Horizon

Chrysler's Omni/Horizon, first introduced in 1978 and priced at an affordable $4500, sold well during the first 18 months it was on the market. But soon after the winter of 1979, problems started showing up.

Omni/Horizons are very vulnerable to cold weather. Constant stalling is usually followed by self-destructing motors and wheel bearings, a failure-prone transmission/differential, and body hardware that is poorly fitted and soon prone to rust. Granted, the Chrysler Corporation extended the warranty to two years or 24,000 miles to cover new or used Omni/ Horizons with wheel-bearing, transmission, oil-pump and distributor defects, but this warranty assistance will be of little help to the buyers of these used vehicles with more than 24,000 miles.

As if the aforementioned defects were not reason enough, bad dealer servicing of Omni/Horizons is another reason to steer clear of the vehicles.

Technical Specifications			
Two-door model:	*1978*	*1979*	*1980*
Wheelbase	99"	97"	97"
Length	163"	173"	173"
Width	66"	67"	67"

Two-door Model	1978	1979	1980
Weight	2100 lb.	2200 lb.	2200 lb.
Standard motor	4 cyl.	4 cyl.	4 cyl.
Gas mileage	32	31	25
Price	$2400	$3100	$4300

Not recommended

Rusting Diagram for Omni/Horizon

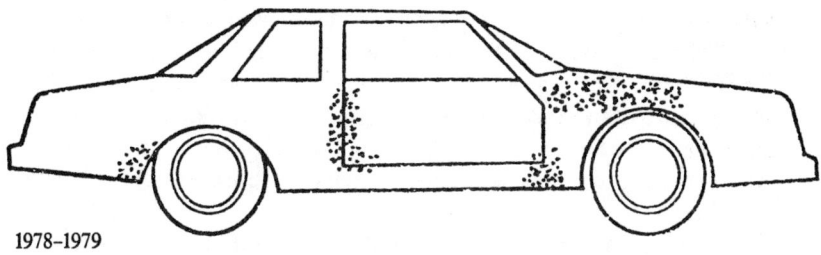

1978–1979

Defect Register

Affected Model	Defect
1978 Dodge Omni and Plymouth Horizon	Possibility that fuel tank may exhibit fuel leakage when completely filled.
	Possibility that the front suspension control arm to ball joint rivet attachments may not be of sufficient strength to withstand high impact loading such as that resulting from wheel hitting a chuck hole at relatively high speed with brakes locked.

AMERICAN MOTORS SUBCOMPACTS

Historically the orphan of the American automobile manufacturers, American Motors has now geared its entire production of new cars to the compact and subcompact models. This marketing strategy hurt the company's sales in 1976 because new- and used-car buyers began returning to the intermediates and large cars when the end of the Arab oil embargo freed up North American oil supplies. However, it still appears that American Motors has the best long-term strategy in pushing its subcompact and compact models. American domestic oil supplies are insufficient if another prolonged oil supply shutdown occurs, and federal gas-mileage regulations for 1981 will certainly add to the popularity of American Motors' small cars. But American Motors may be unable to supply any new models to compete with the innovative small cars that are certain to be introduced by European and American automobile manufacturers.

Without a doubt, American Motors has a good automobile warranty for its new cars. As a result of its liberal warranty policy, many of its used cars may be better maintained than the average used car. Its models seldom change and therefore keep their value over a longer period of time than most other small cars. Parts availability is seldom a problem for cars less than five years old. Used-parts dealers usually won't stock used parts older than five years because there is little demand for them.

Most of American Motors' models are good buys. It may be very difficult to obtain parts for discontinued car lines like the Javelin, AMX, and Ambassador, however. Also, many of the pre-1970 models, particularly the large-sized cars, were poorly designed and transmission failures were common. This is unusual because most domestic and foreign automakers built their best cars before the 1971 model year. For American Motors, car quality improved *after* that same model year.

Servicing used American Motors cars should not be much of a problem. The vehicles are simply made and require no special tools or equipment to maintain. Dealership servicing may not be so easy to find, though, since American Motors has a weak and widely scattered dealership network. Of course with a used car, seeking out dealership servicing is like playing Russian roulette.

Gremlin/Spirit

This is one ugly car. But, like the Volkswagen, Saab, and early Citroëns, cars with unusual bodies can pick up a large following if their mechanical components are not failure-prone. Fortunately, the Gremlin has an excellent past history of providing reliable, inexpensive transportation. Its best features are its motor, electrical system, and automatic transmission. Some of the more troublesome features have been inadequate drum brakes that often veer off in another direction, a weak suspension, and lack of interior space for passenger and driver alike.

Because of the Gremlin's looks and passenger size limitations, prices for used models are very low. The best Gremlin models to buy are the 1975 and 1976 model years that got the early production bugs corrected at the factory.

Spirit, the more handsome but equally sound successor to the Gremlin, first appeared in 1979. It is offered in both four- and six-cylinder models.

Technical Specifications

Two-door model:	1975	1976	1977	1978	1979	1980
Wheelbase	96"	96"	96"	96"	96"	96"
Length	170"	169"	167"	167"	167"	167"
Width	70"	70"	71"	71"	72"	72"
Weight	2800 lb.	2800 lb.	2800 lb.	2800 lb.	2500 lb.	2600 lb.
Standard motor	6 cyl.	6 cyl.	6 cyl.	6 cyl.	4 cyl.	4 cyl.
Gas mileage	20	21	21	18	27	24
Price	$1000	$1500	$1800	$2800	$3500	$4500

Recommended

Rusting Diagrams for Gremlin/Spirit

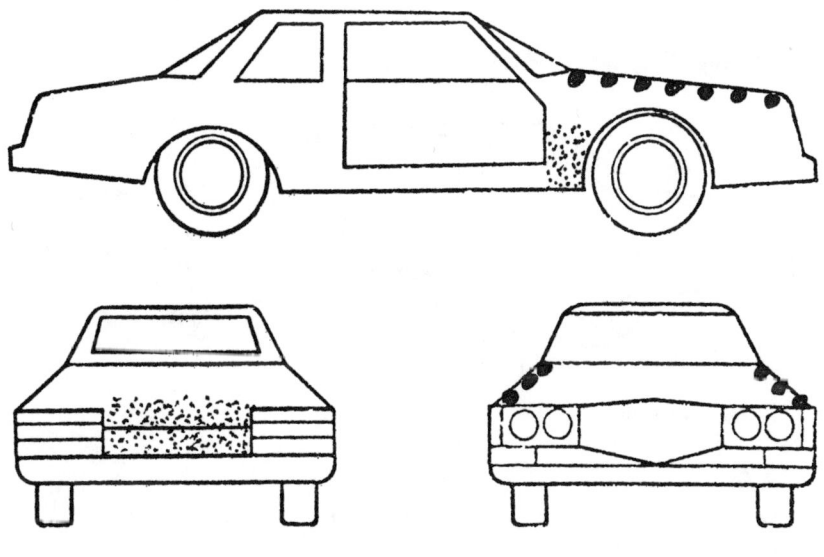

1975-1979

Defect Register

Affected Model
1975 Gremlin,
1976 Hornet

Defect
Possibility that power steering hose was routed close to exhaust manifold. Hose may deteriorate from heat of exhaust manifold.

Pacer

This is another unorthodox car brought out by American Motors to give consumers the interior comfort of a large car with the styling of a subcompact. The car looks like a rolling egg.

When the Pacer was first launched in April of 1975, it created a sensation in the auto industry because of its dramatically different styling. There are serious mechanical and body problems with the Pacer. Consumers have reported poor sealing around the doors and windows allowing water to penetrate the car's interior. Also, Ziebart rustproofers have decided to limit the warranty coverage on the Pacer due to what Ziebart spokesmen have called certain "design problems." Owners have also complained of poor quality in the interior and exterior trim as well as sudden steering lockup.

The Pacer was discontinued in 1980.

Rusting Diagram for Pacer

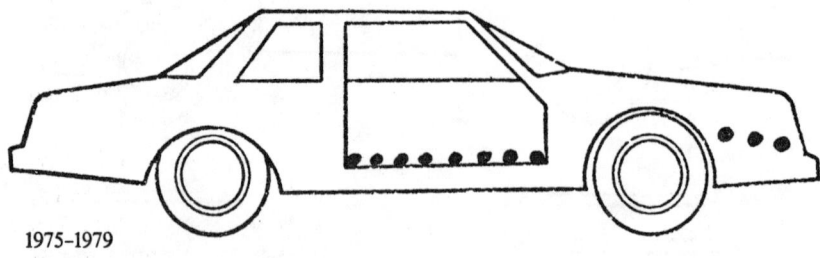

1975-1979

Defect Register

Affected Model
1976 AMC Pacer models built from December 4, 1975 to March 19, 1976

Defect
Rear-seat back hinge latch could fail.

Affected Model
1975 model Pacer passenger cars, with VIN range from A5E667A1000050 to A5C667A218829

Defect
Possible improper installation of a fuel line retainer clip may result in the fuel hose from the fuel line to the fuel pump bearing against the front engine/suspension crossmember, thus causing abrasion and failure of the hose.

Technical Specifications

Two-door model:	1975	1976	1977	1978	1979
Wheelbase	100"	100"	100"	108"	100"
Length	171"	171"	171"	173"	173"
Width	77"	77"	77"	77"	77"
Weight	2995 lb.	3100 lb.	3100 lb.	3000 lb.	3200 lb.
Standard motor	6 cyl.	6 cyl.	6 cyl.	6 cyl.	6 cyl.
Gas mileage	18.5	16	16	16	14
Price	$1400	$1800	$2200	$2800	$3300

Not recommended

GENERAL MOTORS COMPACTS

Citation, Omega, Skylark, and Phoenix

General Motors first put these compact front-wheel-drive models on the market in April of 1979. Called the "X-body" cars, these vehicles benefited from an unprecedented sales success the first six months they were sold. Then word got around that they had serious safety-related and performance-related defects and sales started leveling off.

The 1980 models were plagued by a host of mechanical and body-hardware defects causing constant stalling, chronic motor-oil leaks, sudden motor seizure, automatic-transmission breakdowns (125 Series) and premature rusting caused by peeling paint and the infiltration of water into the passenger compartment.

GM's pricing policies also did a lot to kill X-body sales. Although the model's base price new was only $6000, General Motors and its dealers made sure that many of the X-body cars available were loaded with optional equipment that few motorists wanted or could afford. This pricing mistake inflated the retail selling price of these cars by as much as $2000. So don't be surprised if the used-car price hovers around $5000 for a 1980 Citation.

Depreciation is average for these cars, but parts are not easily obtainable and are costly. Gas mileage is a respectable 23 MPG.

It should be noted that these models all successfully passed the federal government's 35 MPH crash tests when other larger foreign and domestic models failed.

Technical Specifications

Two-door model:	*1980*
Wheelbase	105
Length	177"
Width	68"
Weight	2500 lb.
Standard motor	6 cyl.
Gas mileage	24
Price	$4700

Not recommended

Rusting Diagram for Citation/Omega/Skylark/Phoenix

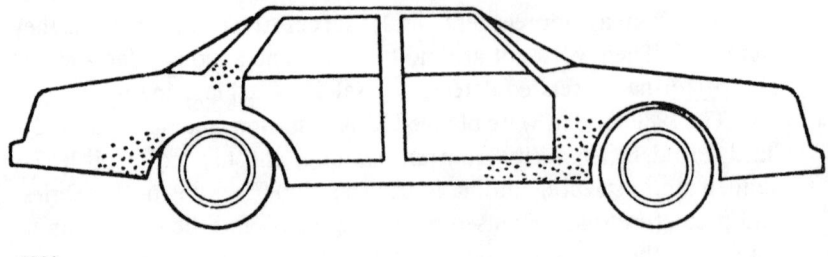

1980

Defect Register

Affected Model
1980 Chevrolet Citation, Pontiac Phoenix, Oldsmobile Omega, Buick Skylark

Defect
Possibility of interference between clutch control cable and brake pipe in area of master cylinder.

Possibility that fuel hoses may be incorrectly positioned and may contact right front drive axle boot while vehicle is being driven. The rotating boot, after a period of time, could wear a hole in fuel hose, resulting in fuel leakage and potential fire in engine compartment.

Nova

The Nova has been one of the most popular compacts in the GM lineup of compact cars. Its popularity explains one of the reasons why the car has a slow rate of depreciation and good availability of parts.

There are no serious mechanical problems with the Nova except for carburetor and ignition foulup caused by GM's emission-control devices. The motor, transmission, brakes, and suspension are generally very reliable for most models. However, the 1977–1978 models equipped with automatic transmissions may have premature transmission failure (around 40,000 miles because of defective 200-series transmissions).

Newspaper want ads are usually full of Nova owners selling their cars privately. The best years are the 1971 and 1974 models.

Technical Specifications

Two-door model:	1975	1976	1977	1978	1979	1980
Wheelbase	111"	111"	111"	111"	111"	111"
Length	194"	197"	197"	197"	194"	194"
Width	72"	72"	72"	72"	72"	72"
Weight	3200 lb.	3300 lb.	3300 lb.	3300 lb.	3200 lb.	3200 lb.
Standard motor	6 cyl.	6 cyl.	6 cyl.	6 cyl.	6 cyl.	6 cyl.
Gas mileage	19.2	21	17	21.2	15.3	18.8
Price	$1700	$2000	$2300	$2900	$3900	$4200

Recommended

Rusting Diagrams for Chevy Nova

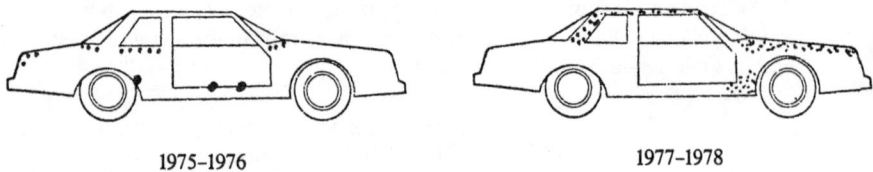

1975–1976   1977–1978

Ventura

Although this is almost the twin of the Chevy Nova, the Ventura does not have the same solid reputation. Pontiac dealers servicing the Ventura have admitted the model has certain body defects that may allow water to leak into the trunk compartment, badly adjusted pollution-control devices causing stalling and hard starting, and premature paint wear on the 1974 model. The Ventura's fuel economy suffers from its motor difficulties and its automatic transmission is covered by GM's "goodwill" warranty extension. This would not be as good a buy as a Chevy Nova.

Technical Specifications same as Nova, page 103

Rusting Diagrams for Pontiac Ventura

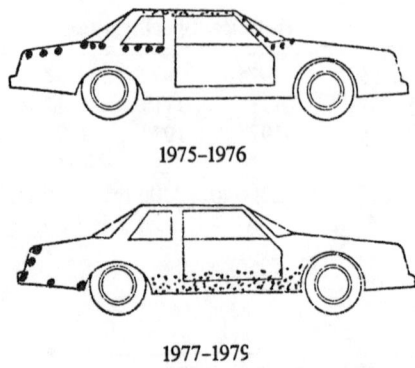

1975–1976

1977–1978

Defect Register

Affected Model	*Defect*
1975 Nova, Omega, Ventura and Apollo passenger car models	The possibility exists whereby the front suspension lower control arm bracket attachments were improperly welded. Failure of these welds could result in loss of vehicle directional control.
1976 Chevrolet Nova, Pontiac Ventura, Oldsmobile Omega and Buick Skylark	Certain of the subject vehicles may have been assembled with plugged or restricted liquid separator pipe assemblies in the fuel tank.
1975 model Apollo, Skylark, Omega and Ventura passenger cars equipped with 260 CID engines	The carburetor throttle cable conduit cover may break at the molded firewall connection, possibly causing a sharp bend in the cable. This results in the strand wires fraying and balling-up inside the conduit cover which could cause the throttle cable to seize in any position. As a result, the vehicle speed could be maintained when the driver's foot is removed from the accelerator and vehicle crash could occur.
1977–1978 Chevrolet Nova, Nova Concours and Nova Custom, Oldsmobile Omega, Buick Skylark, Pontiac Ventura and Pontiac Phoenix	Certain vehicles may be equipped with 7.5-inch rear axle assemblies (coded "O") that have a metal flaw in the axle shaft. The axle shaft may break and allow the tire and wheel assembly to separate from the vehicle.
1977 Chevrolet Nova, Nova Concours, Camaro and Camaro LT equipped with rally road wheels	The center section of the rally road wheels may have been fabricated from an incorrect grade of steel. It is possible that the center section can fatigue and separate from the wheel rim causing a loss of vehicle control and possible vehicle crash without warning to the operator.

Camaro

An excellent pseudo-sports car, the Camaro has the allure of a sleek racing machine while actually providing few of the European racing components serious sports-car enthusiasts expect. GM pulls off a similar trick with its highly successful Corvette "sports" model. Even though the Camaro is not a sports car in the truest sense of the term, popularity makes it one of the most popular compact "sporty-looking" used cars available.

Because of its limited size, the Camaro does not carry rear passengers very well despite what GM may say to the contrary. Most of the mechanical components have no major problems except for the 200-series automatic transmission and front brakes. Minor problems have been reported with paint peeling off post-1976 models. Pontiac's Firebird is almost identical to the Camaro except for some minor styling differences and the availability of different optional equipment.

Both the Camaro and Firebird models are ideal for any motorist wishing to try out a "sports" car for the first time without spending a lot of money on the purchase or at European car-repair shops. Before buying either model, an independent mechanical inspection is prudent, especially if a used Trans Am is being considered.

Technical Specifications

Two-door model:	1975	1976	1977	1978	1979	1980
Wheelbase	108"	108"	108"	108"	108"	108"
Length	195"	197"	197"	197"	198"	198"
Width	74"	74"	74"	74"	74"	74"
Weight	3600 lb.	3600 lb.	3500 lb.	3500 lb.	3600 lb.	3400 lb.
Standard motor	8 cyl.	8 cyl.	8 cyl.	8 cyl.	8 cyl.	8 cyl.
Gas mileage	19	16	16	17	21	20
Price	$2700	$3300	$3500	$3900	$4200	$4700

Recommended

Rusting Diagrams for Camaro

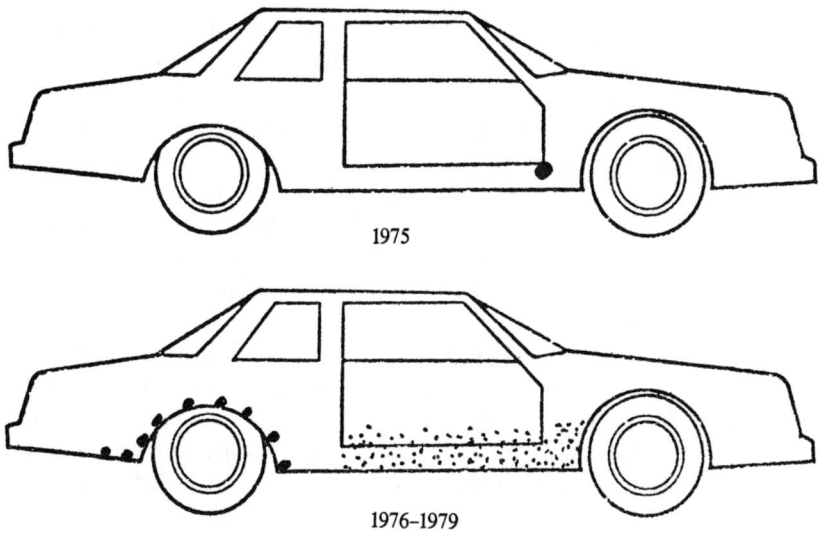

1975

1976–1979

Rusting Diagram for Firebird

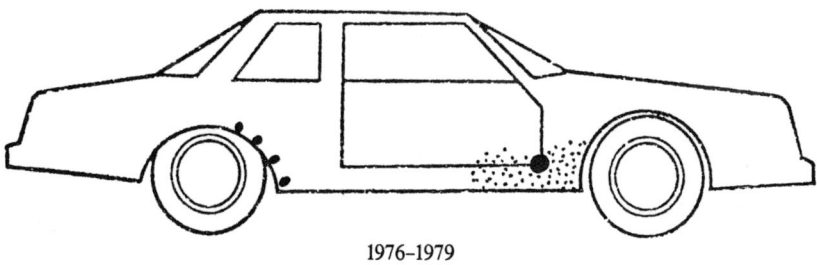

1976–1979

Defect Register

Affected Model
1980 Chevrolet Camaro
and Pontiac Firebird

Defect
Possibility that on certain vehicles the lower control arm ball joint to steering knuckle attaching nut (torque prevailing design) may not have been torqued to specifications.

FORD COMPACTS

Maverick/Comet

Two of the most successful cars Ford marketed, the Maverick and Comet were probably the best-built American cars Ford sold until the models were discontinued in 1978. They require a minimum of maintenance, have a solid six-cylinder motor, and get good gas mileage. Four persons can sit comfortably in both the Maverick and Mercury Comet. Unfortunately, Ford does not appear to have built its cars to last longer than five years. Premature rusting which causes huge perforations in the trunk, on the front and rear doors, and all over the body of Ford's 1975 Maverick/Comets has forced many owners to get rid of their cars long before the mechanical components wear out.

The trunk is very small, rear visibility is partly blocked by the high rear end, and the front idler arms may separate as a result of early corrosion. Brakes, carburetor, and automatic transmissions may wear out prematurely. Purchasing a used Maverick or Comet is wise only if the price is very low and corrosion problems have been ruled out.

Technical Specifications

Two-door model:	1975	1976
Wheelbase	103"	103"
Length	187"	187"
Width	70"	70"
Standard motor	6 cyl.	6 cyl.
Gas mileage	20	19
Price	$1900	$1700

Recommended with reservations

Rusting Diagrams for Maverick/Comet: See p. 88

Granada/Monarch

When the 1974 Arab oil shortage left domestic intermediate and standard car sales in shambles, both Ford and Chrysler had few alternative compact cars to win back the lost customers.

So the Granada/Monarch was rushed into production in the fall of 1974 as a restyled replacement for the 1975 Maverick/Comet. Unfortunately, the model's stylish appearance is marred by serious mechanical and body defects that make this compact both unreliable and expensive to drive.

One of the Granada/Monarch's most serious deficiencies involves the six-cylinder 200 and 250 CID motor. Vehicles manufactured between 1974 and 1978 may have prematurely worn pistons caused by inadequate engine lubrication. This "piston scuffing" is caused by a design defect covered by a special Ford warranty extension on new and used vehicles up to 3 years or 36,000 miles. Naturally, this limitation eliminates all but a very few of the 1978 Granada/Monarch models.

Other defects affect primarily the transmission, starter, and carburetor, thereby transforming what should be an economical car into a "gas guzzler."

Depreciation is average, parts are easily available at moderate prices, and gas mileage with the eight-cylinder varies between 15 and 18 MPG and the six-cylinder gets about 19–21 MPG.

Technical Specifications

Two-door model:	1975	1976	1977	1978	1979	1980
Wheelbase	110"	110"	110"	110"	110"	110"
Length	198"	198"	198"	198"	198"	198"
Width	74"	74"	74"	74"	74"	74"
Weight	3500 lb.	3500 lb.	3500 lb.	3300 lb.	3200 lb.	3200 lb.
Standard motor	6 cyl.	6 cyl.	6 cyl.	6 cyl.	6 cyl.	6 cyl.
Gas mileage	15	15	17	13	17	18
Price	$1700	$2000	$2500	$3200	$4000	$5500

Not recommended

Rusting Diagram for Granada/Monarch

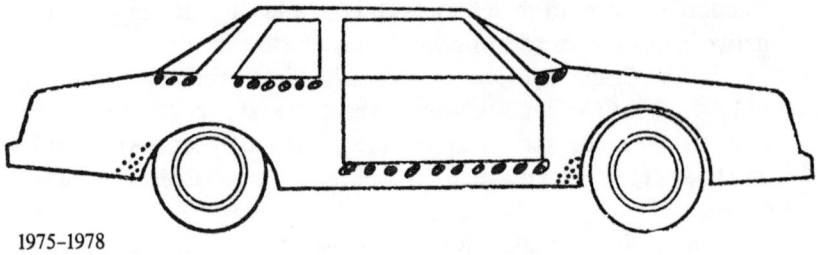

1975–1978

Defect Register

Affected Model
1977 Ford Granada vehicles

Defect
Certain base model 1977 Granadas may not meet the fuel spillage requirements of federal law due to fuel leakage around a deformed fuel filler cap.

1977 Ford Granada, Maverick and Mercury Monarch, Comet vehicles and 1977 Ford F-100-150-250-350 light-duty trucks equipped with manual steering

The manual steering gear recirculating balls may fracture due to improper heat treatment. Fractured recirculating balls will increase steering effort and cause momentary steering hang-up. Continued use of the vehicle will result in a loss of steering control.

1976–1977 Ford Granada and Mercury Monarch two-door vehicles

The shoulder-belt anchorage on vehicles equipped with a continuous loop system may not withstand the specified load requirements of federal law.

1976 Ford Granada and Mercury Monarch

Vehicles may have been built with improperly matched components which secure the front suspension upper arms to the body structure. Such assembly could lead to complete separation of the suspension upper arms and loss of steering.

1979 Ford Granada and Mercury Monarch

Possibility vehicles were produced with brake pushrod to brake pedal retaining pins which were not heat treated as specified.

Mustang

When it was launched in 1965, the first Ford Mustang was an immediate marketing success story: clean sleek lines, little chrome, no rusting problems, good gas mileage, and a dependable motor. Too bad Ford couldn't leave well enough alone. By 1970, the Mustang had been restyled so that it became longer, heavier, expensive to fuel and covered with sheet metal that could rust out within five years. Ford's attempt at transforming the meek, mild-mannered Mustang into a "muscle car" failed, and in 1974 the company reintroduced the Mustang under the Mustang II label.

Since 1970, the Mustang has been one of Ford's most problem-prone cars. The eight-cylinder engine had premature valve-guide wear (supposed to be covered by a secret Ford warranty extension), excessive wheel vibration on the 1974–1976 models said by Ford to be caused by defective Firestone tires and said by Firestone to be caused by defective Ford suspensions, and poor gas mileage that is so much lower than what Ford says one may get that one irate Ford owner was awarded $300 damages when his car got 11 miles instead of the advertised 30 miles to the gallon. The transmission, suspension, and heating system of later Mustangs appear to be inferior to earlier models.

Technical Specifications

Two-door model:	1975	1976	1977	1978	1979	1980
Wheelbase	96"	108"	96"	96"	100"	100"
Length	176"	183"	175"	175"	179"	179"
Width	70"	70"	70"	70"	69"	69"
Weight	3000 lb.	2700 lb.	2700 lb.	2700 lb.	2500 lb.	2500 lb.
Standard motor	6 cyl.	6 cyl.	6 cyl.	6 cyl.	6 cyl.	6 cyl.
Gas mileage	12.6	26	26	20	28	20
Price	$1800	$2300	$2700	$3500	$4200	$4700

Not recommended

Rusting Diagrams for Mustang: See p. 88

Fairmont/Zephyr

Ford put the Fairmont/Zephyr on the American market in the fall of 1977. Its first year's sales were spectacular, due mainly to the car's fuel economy, low price ($4500), and popular station-wagon design.

The Fairmont/Zephyr is a light car that easily zips through urban and expressway traffic conditions. Due to its light weight, the car can out-perform other vehicles in its class and still get a steady 25 MPG.

Despite this excellent fuel economy, the 1979- and 1980-model motors are especially noisy and stalling-prone. Some incidents of motor seizures and transmission failures have also been reported with the four-cylinder motors found in the 1979 and 1980 models. (The four-cylinder is the base engine for the Fairmont, but most of the 1979's and 1980's sold had six-cylinder engines.) Depreciation for all years is below average, parts are easily obtainable and inexpensive, and most mechanical components are quite durable.

Technical Specifications

Two-door model:	1978	1979	1980
Wheelbase	106"	106"	106"
Length	195"	195"	195"
Width	71"	71"	71"
Weight	2900 lb.	2900 lb.	2900 lb.
Standard motor	6 cyl.	6 cyl.	6 cyl.
Gas mileage	21	22	21
Price	$2700	$3200	$4000

Recommended

Rusting Diagram for Fairmont/Zephyr

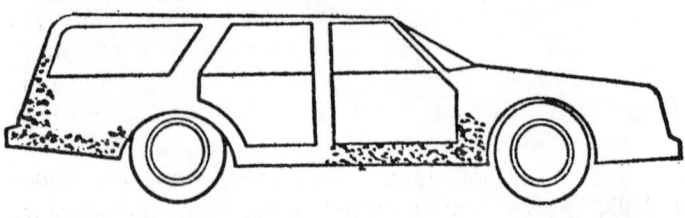

1978–1979

Defect Register

Affected Model	Defect
1978 Ford Fairmont and Mercury Zephyr vehicles equipped with front disc brakes	Some front disc brake rotors may contain cracks and could fracture during vehicle braking resulting in brake pull and affecting vehicle control.
1978 Ford Fairmont and Mercury Zephyr vehicles	Some sedan-type axles were installed in station wagons and vice versa. Sedans might experience early wheel lockup during braking and station wagons would experience reduced braking effectiveness. Station wagons might also fail to meet the brake fade requirements of federal law.
	Possibility vehicles were produced with windshield wiper drive linkages which may fracture due to metal fatigue.
1978 Ford Fairmont and Mercury Zephyr vehicles equipped with automatic transmission and steering column mounted shift controls	The transmission parking pawl may not engage the parking gear when the transmission selector lever is placed in the park position due to excessive freeplay in the shift linkage adjustment. This condition could allow the vehicle to roll free if it is parked without the parking brake engaged.

CHRYSLER COMPACTS

Valiant

Undoubtedly, the best used compact car on the market is the Plymouth Valiant. It has remained essentially the same since it was first introduced. Parts are plentiful and cheap. Depreciation is so slow that the car may actually increase in value. Gas mileage is good yet there is adequate room for five adults and a rear trunk that can handle more than the average load of baggage. The only problem with the Valiant is that the newest one on the used-car lot will be a 1976 model, since they were discontinued at that time.

Valiants are simple cars to repair. Equipped with a six-cylinder motor that is the closest invention yet to a perpetual-motion machine, the car requires very little periodic maintenance. The only major repairs that a Valiant could require would be the occasional changing of the rusted-out front fenders every four years or so and the examining and replacing of the brakes that have a tendency to lock during emergency braking. There is also a chronic stalling problem, which can easily be solved by replacing the ballast resistor. This is the ideal car for a family of five that does not wish to spend any extra money for the additional room that an intermediate may offer.

Technical Specifications

Two-door model:	1975	1976
Wheelbase	108"	108"
Length	195"	195"
Width	71"	71"
Weight	3000 lb.	3000 lb.
Standard motor	6 cyl.	6 cyl.
Gas mileage	21.6	21.6
Price	$1900	$2300
Recommended		

Dart

Identical in most ways to the Valiant, the Dart was marketed through Chrysler Dodge dealers, while the Valiant was given to Chrysler Plymouth dealers. This way the manufacturer can split the market with what is essentially the same car.

Despite the similarities of the two Chrysler models, Dart owners have reported a number of disturbing defects that have not shown up in the Valiant model. For example, Darts have water leaks (Chrysler products have always had water leaks, or so it seems), transmission clutch failures, and electronic ignition short-circuiting. Many owners complain of premature brake wear and brake locking, similar to the Valiant. Nevertheless, the Dart has practically all the advantages of the Valiant and one would be hard-pressed to find any other used car with as much quality in its construction.

Used-car prices for both the Valiant and Dart are low because Chrysler dropped the two models from production in 1976. This is only technically true, though, because Chrysler replaced the Dart and Valiant with the Aspen and Volaré. Both of these replacements have practically the same characteristics as the cars they have replaced, although they are less reliable. Used parts should never be a problem.

Technical Specifications

Two-door model:	1975	1976
Wheelbase	111"	111"
Length	203"	201"
Width	69"	72"
Weight	3000 lb.	3000 lb.
Standard motor	6 cyl.	6 cyl.
Gas mileage	20.4	20
Price	$1900	$2300
Recommended		

Rusting Diagram for Dart/Valiant

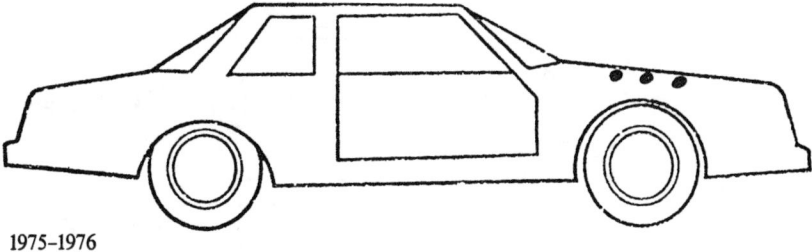

1975-1976

Volaré/Aspen

The Volaré/Aspen, introduced in 1976, was a restyled version of the reliable and economical Valiant/Dart models equipped with the legendary "slant-six" engine. Unfortunately, in this case "new" did not mean "improved." Although Chrysler poured millions into new sheet metal to make the car attractive, the vehicle's mechanical components and body hardware were not as well made as in the Valiant/Dart models.

The early Volaré/Aspen models have become infamous for their chronic stalling, rust-prone fenders, water leaks in the passenger compartment, and troublesome transmission/differentials. These problems, however, have been encountered most frequently with the 1976-1978 models. The 1979 and 1980 Volaré/Aspen models seem somewhat improved. Chrysler has extended the warranty to cover fender rusting, stalling and transmission/differential failures.

Depreciation is rapid, parts are easily obtainable at moderate cost (front fenders excepted), and gas consumption varies considerably.

Technical Specifications

Two-door model:	1976	1977	1978	1979	1980
Wheelbase	109"	109"	109"	109"	109"
Length	198"	198"	198"	198"	198"
Width	74"	74"	73"	73"	73"
Weight	3500 lb.	3500 lb.	3300 lb.	3100 lb.	3200 lb.
Standard motor	6 cyl.	6 cyl.	6 cyl.	6 cyl.	6 cyl.
Gas mileage	17	17	13	17	18
Price	$1500	$2100	$2800	$3400	$4200

Not recommended 1976–1978, and use caution when purchasing 1979–1980 models

Rusting Diagram for Volaré/Aspen

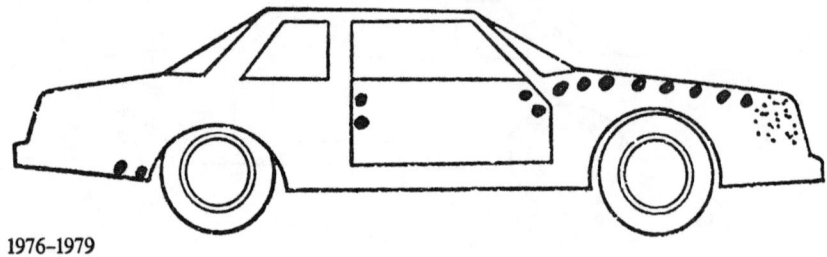

1976–1979

Defect Register

Affected Model

1976–1977 Dodge Aspen and Plymouth Volaré and 1978 Dodge Diplomat and Chrysler LeBaron vehicles

Defect

The steel brake tubes may be subject to corrosion from battery acid. Also the front brake hoses may become brittle and crack in sustained extreme cold temperatures.

1976 Volaré, Aspen, Fury and Coronet Charger passenger cars

The involved vehicles were equipped with an incorrect EGR vacuum amplifier.

1976 Dodge Aspen and Plymouth Volaré station wagons built from November, 1975, through mid February, 1976

The tire pressure placards incorrectly specify front-tire pressure as 22 p.s.i. instead of 24 p.s.i. as required for maximum load conditions by federal law.

Affected Model	Defect
1976 Plymouth Volaré and Fury, 1976 Dodge Aspen, Charger and Coronet and 1976 Chrysler Cordoba vehicles with power brakes	The power-brake booster may contain silencer pads that restrict the input air due to excessive silencer material density. This can cause braking action delay and result in increased stopping distances.
1976 two-door model Plymouth Volaré and Dodge Aspen passenger vehicles built from November, 1975, through early February, 1976	The driver and front outboard passenger seat belts may not engage in the locked position when extracted for occupant use.
1979 Plymouth Volaré	Possibility that three engine compartment fuel line hoses are made of neoprene rubber compound, which may deteriorate with continued exposure to underhood temperatures.

AMERICAN MOTORS COMPACTS

Hornet/Concord

In introducing the Hornet in 1970, American Motors hoped to improve its reputation with consumers who had been turned off by the failure-prone Rambler. The plan worked and thousands of new Hornets were sold during the first few months of its introduction.

American Motors has not changed the Hornet's styling or its engineering very much over the years. This is one of the main reasons why the car has attracted so many buyers. Parts availability is good, depreciation about average, and interior space is more than adequate for five adults. Mechanically, the Hornet has been improved since 1975 when many owners complained of poorly performing front brakes, transmission and carburetor failures. However, in subsequent models minor defects would still be encountered with the suspension, brakes, and carburetor leading the list of problem components.

The Hornet/Concord represents a good used-car buy because of its low resale price and anticipated reliability, and 5-year rust warranty.

Technical Specifications

Two-door model:	1975	1976	1977	1978	1979	1980
Wheelbase	108"	108"	108"	108"	108"	108"
Length	186"	186"	186"	186"	186"	184"
Width	71"	71"	71"	71"	71"	71"
Weight	2880 lb.	2900 lb.	3000 lb.	3000 lb.	2880 lb.	2700 lb.
Standard motor	6 cyl.	6 cyl.	6 cyl.	6 cyl.	6 cyl.	6 cyl.
Gas mileage	21.6	19	20	17	26	21
Price	$1900	$2400	$2900	$3300	$3700	$4600

Recommended

Rusting Diagram for Hornet/Concord

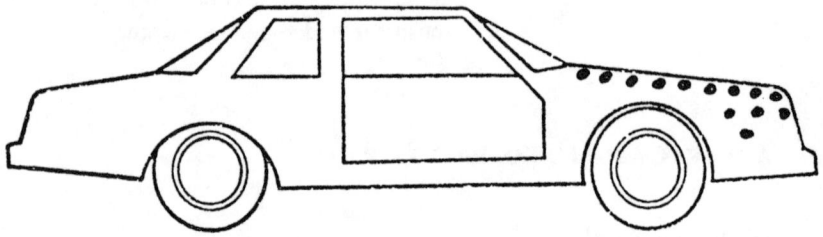

1975–1980

Defect Register

Affected Model
1977 AMC Gremlin equipped with four-cyl. engines and within the serial number ranges A7C464G189369 to A7M464G230674 and A7M464G716985 to A7C464G728298

Defect
The accelerator cable on four-cylinder engines has a plastic sleeve of incorrect length which could jam when the accelerator pedal is depressed fully to the floor causing the throttle to remain in a fully opened position when the accelerator pedal is released.

Affected Model	Defect
1978 AMC Gremlin vehicles equipped with four-cylinder engines and four-speed manual transmissions. The serial number ranges of the affected vehicles are: A8M464G100021 through A8M464G355129 and A8M464G700005 through A8M464G813059	The instrument panel wiring harness may contact and be chafed by the clutch linkage during normal vehicle operation. An electrical fire can result if the harness wires become shorted.
1975 Model Pacer, Hornet and Gremlin passenger cars	Possibility exists that the jack assemblies on the above units are of substandard quality.
1975 model Hornet and Gremlin passenger cars	Possibility exists that units are equipped with the front suspension strut assembly containing nuts of substandard quality.
1980 AMC Eagle	Possibility that half-shaft assembly on right or left side of front-wheel-drive mechanism may develop fracture near its inboard attachment point.

GENERAL MOTORS INTERMEDIATES

Chevelle/Malibu

This model has been one of Chevrolet's most reliable intermediates. Motor, suspension, and manual transmission receive excellent ratings from Chevelle/Malibu owners. Brakes, automatic transmissions, paint, and an inadequate interior ventilation system are the areas most owners complained about. Parts availability is excellent. Depreciation is below average. Some of the early 1966–1971 models could have defective motor supports and inadequate body sealing allowing carbon monoxide gas to seep into the passenger compartment. Both of these defects precipitated safety recall campaigns. General Motors has extended the warranty on the 200-series automatic transmission and paint defects. These problems have been especially severe on the 1976–1980 models. Also 231 CID V-6 and 305 CID V-8 motors are particularly failure prone.

Technical Specifications

Four-door model:	1975	1976	1977
Wheelbase	116"	112"	112"
Length	210"	206"	206"
Width	76"	76"	76"
Weight	3680 lb.	3700 lb.	3600 lb.
Standard motor	6 cyl.	6 cyl.	6 cyl.
Gas mileage	19.2	20	20
Price	$1800	$2400	$2700

Recommended

Rusting Diagram for Chevrolet Chevelle

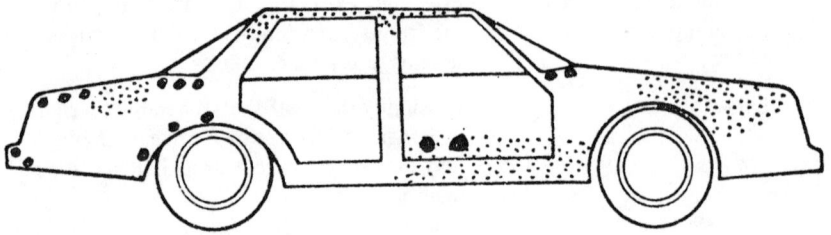

1975-1977

LeMans

Don't let the name mislead you—the LeMans has nothing in common with the famous French racing circuit. In 1970, it made its first appearance on the market. The car never did sell very well because of tough competition like the Chevelle/Malibu and Ford Torino. Owners complained of poor rear visibility, but this was a common complaint with most intermediates until the fastback styling was brought under control in 1974. In the 1975 models, paint peeling and rusting were the most serious body problem. Both the transmission and motor were improved in the 1975 model, but persistent malfunctioning of the carburetor and pollution-control system was left uncorrected.

Owners may claim compensation from General Motors for 1976-1979 paint and transmission problems. Both defects are covered by GM's extended warranty.

Technical Specifications

Four-door model:	1975	1976	1977	1978	1979
Wheelbase	116"	112"	112"	108"	108"
Length	212"	208"	208"	199"	199"
Width	77"	77"	77"	72"	72"
Weight	3800 lb.	3700 lb.	3600 lb.	3300 lb.	3200 lb.
Standard motor	V-8	6 cyl.	6 cyl.	6 cyl.	6 cyl.
Gas mileage	19.2	17	16	18	20
Price	$2700	$2500	$2900	$3700	$4000

Not recommended

Defect Register

Affected Model	*Defect*
1975 Chevrolet Monte Carlo, El Camino, Chevelle; Oldsmobile Cutlass series (except Oldsmobile Supreme Wagons); Pontiac LeMans, Grand LeMans, Grand AM (except LeMans Wagons); Buick Century and Regal (except Century Wagons); and GMC Sprints	Certain Buick "B" or Oldsmobile "O" type rear axles were assembled with side-thrust plates that were not hardened, which could allow the rollers to wear through and could allow separation of the wheel and axle assembly from the vehicle, with potential vehicle crash.
1977 Chevrolet, Chevelle, Monte Carlo, El Camino, Nova and Camaro 1977 Oldsmobile Cutlass, 88, 98 and Omega 1977 Pontiac Bonneville, Catalina, Grand Prix, LeMans and Ventura 1977 Buick Skylark, Century Regal, LeSabre and Electra 1977 GMC Sprint	Possible separation of the steering intermediate shaft at the flexible coupling, which can result in loss of steering control.

Affected Model	Defect
1977 Chevrolet Monte Carlo, Malibu, Pontiac, LeMans, Grand Prix, Oldsmobile Cutlass, Buick Century and Regal	Possibility rear axle shaft may have flaw in metal. As a result, shaft may break, which could allow tire and wheel assembly to separate from vehicle.
1978 Pontiac LeMans, Chevrolet Malibu and Monte Carlo	The rear brake wheel cylinder retainer may not be properly installed. Should the retainer disengage, the wheel cylinder could move outward causing a loss of brake fluid and loss of rear brakes.

CHRYSLER INTERMEDIATES

LeBaron/Diplomat

Chrysler's LeBaron/Diplomat is nothing more than a Volaré/Aspen in disguise. Created by Chrysler's stylists from the Volaré/Aspen frame and mechanical components, this vehicle shares all of the mechanical and body deficiencies of its counterpart.

Chronic stalling with both the six- and eight-cylinder motor is a common problem on models equipped with optional lean-burn computer. Faulty ignition ballast resistors and carburetor cups also contribute to the stalling problem. LeBaron/Diplomat is also prone to transmission/differential failures between 24,000 and 36,000 miles.

Most of the body hardware deficiencies concern the premature rusting of the doors and front fenders as well as the premature peeling off of the paint.

Technical Specifications

Four-door model:	1978	1979	1980
Wheelbase	113"	113"	113"
Length	204"	204"	206"
Width	73"	73"	73"
Weight	4100 lb.	3300 lb.	3400 lb.
Standard motor	6 cyl.	6 cyl.	6 cyl.
Gas mileage	14	16	19
Price	$2800	$3700	$4500

Not recommended

Rusting Diagram for LeBaron/Diplomat

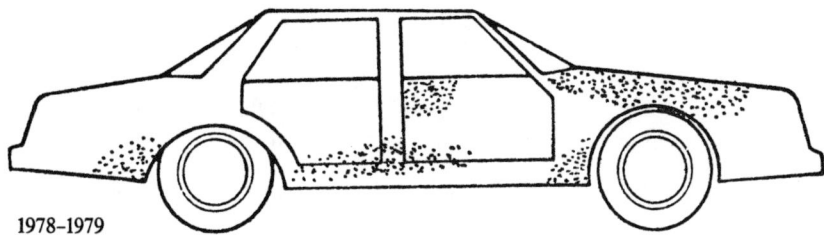

1978–1979

Defect Register

Affected Model
1978 Chrysler Cordoba and LeBaron, Plymouth Fury, Volaré and Caravelle and Dodge Diplomat, Aspen, Monaco and Magnum XE vehicles.

Defect
Vehicles were built with ignition timing that is not compatible with the installed spark control computer so that exhaust emissions do not comply with federal law.

GENERAL MOTORS LARGE CARS

Impala/Caprice

These two models sold by General Motors are typical of what Europeans often say is distasteful about American cars. They are large, full of options, wasteful with gas, and designed primarily for drivers who use high-speed expressways rather than the small secondary roads one finds all over Europe. The Caprice and Impala may not give their owners the true feel of the road or provide the high performance that European cars do, but the driver of one of these large American cars knows the ride will be comfortable, fast, and trouble-free. For this reason, GM has remained the leader in the sales of large and luxury cars.

Both these models have good parts availability and a steady depreciation rate. Servicing is a snap and parts are very inexpensive. Problems have been reported with the brakes, motor mounts, Rochester carburetor sealing of the rear passenger compartment from carbon monoxide fumes, automatic transmission, and paint peeling. The transmission and paint defects have affected post-1976 models; the other safety-related defects affected models manufactured before 1973. Despite these problems, both models represent good used-car buys.

Technical Specifications

Four-door model:	1975	1976	1977
Wheelbase	121"	121"	116"
Length	222"	222"	212"
Width	79"	79"	79"
Weight	4666 lb.	4300 lb.	3700 lb.
Standard motor	V-8	8 cyl.	V-8
Gas mileage	15.7	17	15
Price	$1500	$1000	$1300

Recommended

Rusting Diagram for Chevrolet Impala/Caprice

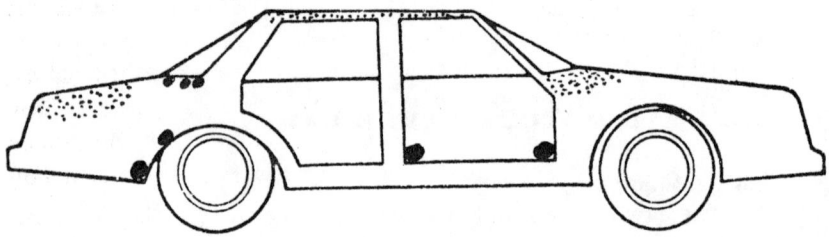

1975–1977

Defect Register

Affected Model
1981 Chevrolet Impala and Caprice, Buick Electra and LeSabre

Defect
Possibility that certain vehicles equipped with gasoline engines may have been assembled with a brake pedal support bracket designed for use in diesel engine equipped vehicles. The incorrect bracket causes brakes to remain partially applied, resulting in overheating and reduction of effectiveness.

Delta 88/Royale

The Oldsmobile Delta 88 is one of the less expensive Oldsmobiles on the market. For this reason it may make a good alternative choice if a similar Pontiac or Buick model is unavailable. Like similar large cars, gas economy is poor, but usable interior space is maximized. Its eight-cylinder motor and brakes give this Oldsmobile a stability at high speeds that would easily put Ford to shame (Ford has a high-speed stability problem).

One of the amazing things about the Delta 88 is its strong resale value. Of course, it's no secret that the Oldsmobile models have a slow rate of depreciation, can be serviced easily and inexpensively, and need few major repairs.

As with other GM models, the Oldsmobile line began to lose much of its quality after the 1976 model year. The Delta and Cutlass models have been particularly affected by failures of the brakes, automatic transmission, and paint peeling away leaving large splotches all over the car. Although GM has extended the warranty to compensate victims of these defects, getting that compensation can sometimes prove to be so much of a hassle that many new car owners abandoned their claims. If you can get a 1976 or earlier Oldsmobile at a fair price, grab it. They are truly not making them like they used to. More recent Oldsmobile models are recommended only if the body and 200-series transmission have been thoroughly checked out.

Technical Specifications

Four-door model:	1976	1977	1978	1979	1980
Wheelbase	124"	119"	108"	108"	108"
Length	227"	220"	199"	199"	199"
Width	79"	77"	72"	72"	72"
Weight	4500 lb.	4000 lb.	3300 lb.	3200 lb.	3300 lb.
Standard motor	V-8 (455)	V-8	V-8	6 cyl.	6 cyl.
Gas mileage	12.7	19	17	22	21
Price	$2500	$2900	$3400	$4000	$5100

Recommended

Rusting Diagram for Oldsmobile Delta 88/Royale

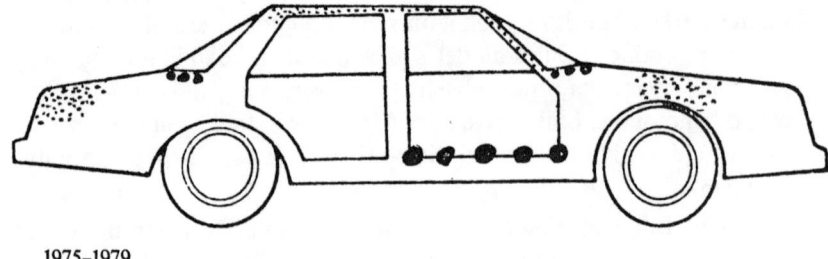

1975–1979

Le Sabre/Electra/Century

Buick dealers sell these overpriced but reliable large-sized cars. They, too, have all the advantages and disadvantages of large cars; plenty of usable interior space, high-speed stability, strong motor, and a good suspension system. Of course, gas mileage is likely to be a problem, but that is to be expected of all large cars.

As these models were widely distributed because of their popularity, parts availability is no problem. Cost of parts, however, may be high since these Buick models appear to have parts that cost more than their Chevrolet and Pontiac counterparts. Automatic transmission defects and paint peeling are a constant problem with these models. Even the Pontiac Catalina and Bonneville have not escaped the ravages of GM's paint problems. Consumer demand for these cars has gone down, so it should not be difficult to bargain down the price of a good used model with most sellers.

Technical Specifications

Four-door model:	1975	1976	1977	1978	1979	1980
Wheelbase	124"	124"	116"	116"	116"	116"
Length	224"	227"	218"	218"	217"	217"
Width	79"	79"	77"	77"	77"	75"
Weight	4600 lb.	4200 lb.	3900 lb.	3600 lb.	3600 lb.	3500 lb.
Standard motor	V-8	V-8	V-8	V-8	6 cyl.	6 cyl.
Gas mileage	16.2	15	18	17	17	14
Price	$2600	$3000	$3500	$4000	$5000	$6300

Recommended

Rusting Diagram for Buick Le Sabre

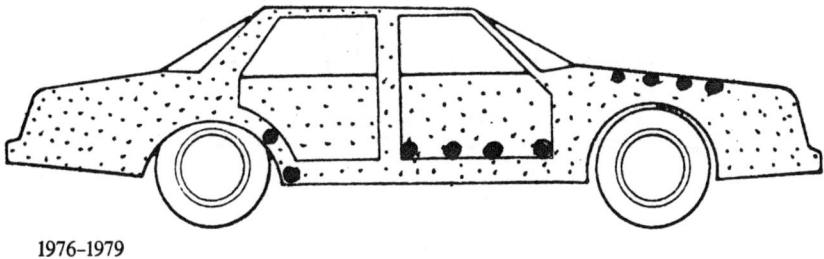

1976–1979

Defect Register

Affected Model
1976 Buick Century, Regal, LeSabre, Electra and Riviera except Century Wagon and Estate Wagon. 1976 Pontiac Le Mans; Le Mans Sport Coupe, Catalina, Bonneville, and Grand Prix except station wagons

Defect
The rear proportioning module of the brake combination valve may have been improperly machined and brake fluid pressure to the rear brakes may be blocked off.

FORD LARGE CARS

Custom/Galaxie

If it were not for Ford's serious corrosion problems, the Custom and Galaxie would be the best models available in the large-car category. Both these models could easily offer the used-car purchaser a cheaper alternative to some of the more expensive GM intermediates and large cars.

Ford's mechanical problems do not seem to have affected the Custom and Galaxie models to any great extent. The only recurring problems seem to be premature valve-guide wear in the eight-cylinder motor, and a tendency for the car to fishtail when rounding curves at high speeds. Yet, these same two problems have been reported with other Ford models, so it does not seem that the Custom or Galaxie should be criticized too harshly.

The rusting problems associated with Ford used-car models have been alleviated since Ford's introduction of an anti-corrosion treatment in 1978. But when buying earlier years it is best to keep in mind that an attractive "bargain" may be offset by severe rusting.

Technical Specifications

Four-door model:	1975	1976	1977	1978
Wheelbase	121"	121"	121"	121"
Length	219"	219"	219"	219"
Width	79"	79"	79"	79"
Weight	4631 lb.	4631 lb.	3600 lb.	3500 lb.
Standard motor	V-8	V-8	6 cyl.	6 cyl.
Gas mileage	14.6	17.1	17	18
Price	$1500	$1700	$2300	$3000
Recommended				

CHRYSLER LARGE CARS

Fury

This is one large-sized car made by Chrysler that still gives good value to its owner. It compares favorably with similar sized cars made by GM and Ford and probably represents the best large car Chrysler has made during the last decade. Only the American Motors Ambassador offers as much quality in the same size of car. Fury models are so popular that they have been used extensively by police forces and taxi companies. Owners report the traditional brake, suspension, and water leakage problems. Some minor electrical problems have also persisted. Despite these diverse defects, the Fury is an excellent used-car buy. The 1976–1978 models should be avoided, however, since they had excessive rusting of the front fenders and electrical problems that caused frequent hard starting and stalling. The 1975 and 1980 models are the best.

Technical Specifications

Four-door model:	1975	1976	1977	1978	1979	1980
Wheelbase	120"	118"	117"	115"	—	119"
Length	222"	218"	218"	213"	—	220"
Width	79"	78"	78"	78"	78"	78"
Weight	4460 lb.	3800 lb.	3800 lb.	3700 lb.	3500 lb.	3400 lb.

Four-door model:	1975	1976	1977	1978	1979	1980
Standard motor	V-8(313)	V-8(318)	V-8(318)	6 cyl.	6 cyl.	6 cyl.
Gas mileage	15.6	14	18	19	17	18
Price	$3000	$1900	$2600	$3400	$4500	$5800

Recommended

Rusting Diagram for Plymouth Fury

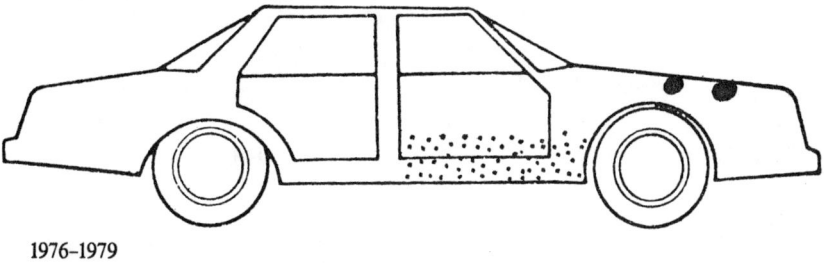

1976–1979

Defect Register

Affected Model
1978 Plymouth Fury and Volaré, Dodge Monaco, Aspen, Diplomat and Magnum XE and Chrysler Cordoba and LeBaron vehicles equipped with tilt steering columns

Defect
The steering column coupling roll pin retaining notch was machined too deep. The roll pin may loosen allowing an disengagement of the steering shaft and column coupling resulting in a loss of steering capability.

1976 Plymouth Fury and Dodge Coronet/Charger vehicles equipped with Firestone F78-15 Deluxe Champion Sup-R-Belt white stripe or blackwall tires. Vehicles were built from early to mid-February, 1976

The suspect tires were manufactured with an incorrect body ply fabric in the sidewall area.

1975 Fury and Coronet passenger cars equipped with the 318 CID, two-barrel engine

Vehicles were inadvertently built with the incorrect engine timing, vehicle emission control information label and orifice spark advance control valve.

Affected Model	Defect
1975 Intermediate (Fury, Coronet and Charger S.E.) and Full Size (Gran Fury and Monaco) passenger cars equipped with the 318 engine	Vehicles to have the ignition timing changed from dead center (D.C.) to two degrees after D.C. and the correct emission label installed.
1975 Intermediate Models (Fury and Coronet) and full-sized models (Gran Fury and Monaco), police and taxi passenger cars	Loosening and ultimately loss of the right front strut nut can occur under severe service conditions and can lead to abrupt loss of directional control.
1976 Compact (Valiant and Dart) Intermediate (Fury, Coronet, and Charger S.E.) and full size (Gran Fury, Monaco, and Chrysler) passenger cars equipped with 360, 400, or 440 CID, four-barrel engines	Vehicles may experience a carburetor step-up piston-sticking condition.

GENERAL MOTORS LUXURY CARS

Monte Carlo/Grand Prix

This is one large car that has been classed in the luxury-car category because of its popularity and the accumulated cost of all the options available. The Monte Carlo was originally introduced as a Chevrolet intermediate for car buyers without the financial resources to purchase one of GM's higher-priced models like the Grand Prix.

Monte Carlo owners report few problems with their cars, except for radial tire defects and crankshaft/camshaft failures. Depreciation is very slow and parts availability is excellent.

Monte Carlo owners have complained about GM's automatic transmissions failing and the premature peeling of the paint. After threatening to take GM and its dealers to small claims court, many of these problems have been rectified by General Motors warranty extension programs that GM insists upon calling "goodwill."

Technical Specifications

Four-door model:	1975	1976	1977	1978	1979	1980
Wheelbase	116"	116"	116"	108"	108"	108"
Length	218"	218"	218"	204"	200"	200"
Width	77"	77"	71"	71"	71"	71"
Weight	4430 lb.	4430 lb.	4430 lb.	4430 lb.	4430 lb.	4430 lb.
Standard motor	V-8	V-8	V-8	V-8	V-8	6 cyl.
Gas mileage	15.6	16	16	17	17	20
Price	$2500	$2700	$3000	$3500	$4300	$5000

Recommended

Rusting Diagram For Chevrolet Monte Carlo

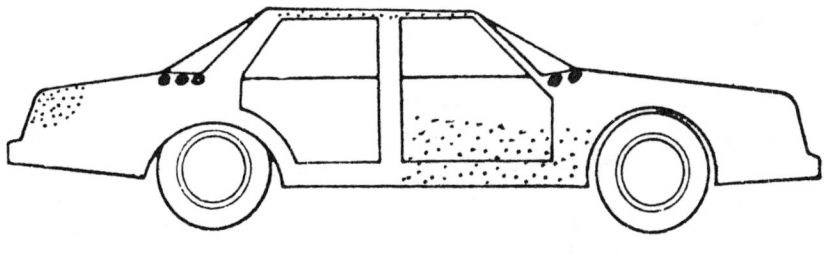

1975-1979

FORD LUXURY CARS

Thunderbird

 Believe it or not, the Thunderbird was once the Corvette's most serious competitor. That was a long time ago, and since that time GM has adopted a fiberglass body for the Corvette, whereas Ford's Thunderbird rarely lasts five years without falling apart.
 Owners call the Thunderbird "Ford's Luxury Lemon" and in some of Ford's own secret documents, the car is described in similar terms. Electrical problems, paint mismatching, poor dealer servicing, defective motors, and a host of other problems are noted by Ford's quality control people. Depreciation is rapid, parts availability and cost is average, and gas economy is about average for a car of this size and weight. All things considered, a used Thunderbird is not recommended.

Technical Specifications

Four-door model:	1975	1976	1977	1978	1979	1980
Wheelbase	117"	117"	117"	114"	113"	108"
Length	215"	215"	215"	215"	215"	200"
Width	78"	78"	78"	78"	74"	74"
Weight	4700 lb.	4700 lb.	4700 lb.	4000 lb.	3900 lb.	3200 lb.
Standard motor	V-8	V-8	V-8	V-8	V-8	V-8
Gas mileage	11.3	11.9	11.6	12	14	18
Price	$2300	$2600	$3000	$3400	$4600	$5300

Not recommended

Defect Register

Affected Model

1977 Ford, Mercury, LTD II, Cougar, Thunderbird, Ranchero, F-100-150-250 and F-350 vehicles equipped with 351 or 400 CID Cleveland engines

1977–1978 Ford vehicles and 1977 Mercury, LTD II, Cougar, Thunderbird, Granada, Monarch, Versailles Lincoln and Mark V vehicles equipped with tilt steering columns

1975 model Ford, Torino, Thunderbird, Mercury, Meteor, Montego, Cougar. Lincoln and

Defect

Certain Cleveland engines may experience fuel leakage at the rubber hose connecting the fuel inlet tube to the carburetor fuel filter. A fuel leakage in the engine compartment creates the danger of fire.

Some tilt steering columns contain transmission control inserts (gear selector pointers) that were intended for use in 1978 model trucks. Use of these inserts could allow the engine to be started with the shift selector positioned between neutral (N) and drive (D) and the transmission in drive. There is a possibility of starting the vehicle with the transmission in drive creating the possibility of a frontal collision.

1) A carburetor fuel inlet cross-channel "O" ring on the sealing plug could be pushed out during vehicle operation, allowing gasoline to be discharged onto the engine. Should this

Affected Model	Defect
Mark IV passenger cars, E-250 Econolines and F-150, F-250, F-350 Light Trucks equipped with a 460 CID engine and a 4350-4V carburetor	occur, the danger of underhood fire could exist. 2) Carburetor secondary throttle stop levers may have been incorrectly stamped. Under certain conditions this could allow engine "runaway" due to secondary throttle plates being held open. Under operating conditions, acceleration of the vehicle to excessive speed may occur.
1981 Ford LTD, Mercury Marquis, Lincoln Mark VI	Possibility that on certain vehicles a "start-in-reverse" condition may exist due to neutral startswitch.

European Models

BRITISH LEYLAND

Consumers are angry with British Leyland. In spite of England's reputation for making exceptional sports cars that sold for reasonable prices, BLM reversed the trend and now sells defect-prone cars for unreasonable prices. British Leyland is not to be blamed entirely for this turnabout. The automobile industry in Great Britain has the same reputation for poor workmanship in its moderately priced new cars.

England's British Leyland auto manufacturer answers the important consumer question, "Can an automobile manufacturer that consistently makes inferior vehicles, with a parts-replacement system that moves by stagecoach, and a dealer network that is practically nonexistent, survive and still be profitable?" with both a yes and a no.

BLM is in pitiful shape, as is most of the British automobile industry. British Leyland, however, has suffered a steeper decline in sales and reputation than most of its English compatriots, owing primarily to the misjudging of the American foreign-car market by its former chief executive, Lord Stokes. Consequently, British Leyland is surviving, but just barely.

The Austin Marina is the English revenge against its former American colonies. It uses the same "infernal combustion" engine that generations of MG owners loved to hate. The Jaguar six-cylinder is a waste of money, while the Jaguar V-12 is doubly wasteful.

The Triumph is the ideal car to teach young sports-car enthusiasts the therapeutic value of walking. It's an all-around bad car that has all the problems endemic to British Leyland's automotive decline.

British Leyland's warranty performance, dealer network and parts availability have been rated poor by many owners driving its products. Marina owners complain of poor dealer servicing, transmission, engine, and brake defects. MG owners gripe about fragile convertible tops, excessive oil consumption, and high service charges. Jaguar owners dislike waiting for parts and have reported that the engines of some recent Jaguar models often hesitate and stall.

None of the British Leyland models are good used-car investments. Europe, Japan and the United States have better cars on the used-car market.

Technical Specifications

Austin Marina:	1976	1977
Wheelbase	96"	96"
Length	172"	172"
Width	69"	69"
Weight	2252 lb.	2200 lb.
Standard motor	4 cyl.	4 cyl.
Gas mileage	20	21
Price	$1300	$1600

Not recommended

MGB:	1976	1977	1978	1979	1980
Wheelbase	91.1"	91"	91"	91"	91"
Length	158.2"	141"	141"	141"	144"
Width	59.9"	54"	54"	54"	54"
Weight	2340 lb.	2300 lb.	2336 lb.	2300 lb.	2338 lb.
Standard motor	4 cyl.	4 cyl.	4 cyl.	4 cyl.	4 cyl.
Gas mileage	25	25.3	24	25.9	26.3
Price	$3600	$4500	$5300	$6000	$7000

Not recommended

Triumph:	1976	1977	1978	1979	1980
Wheelbase	88"	88"	86.4"	85.1"	85.1"
Length	162"	162"	162"	162"	162"
Width	58"	58"	58"	58"	58"
Weight	2600 lb.	2600 lb.	2650 lb.	2700 lb.	2776 lb.
Standard motor	4 cyl.	4 cyl.	4 cyl.	4 cyl.	4 cyl.
Gas mileage	26	25	25	26	27
Price	$800	$1000	$1300	$1900	$2200

Not recommended

Rusting Diagram for British Leyland

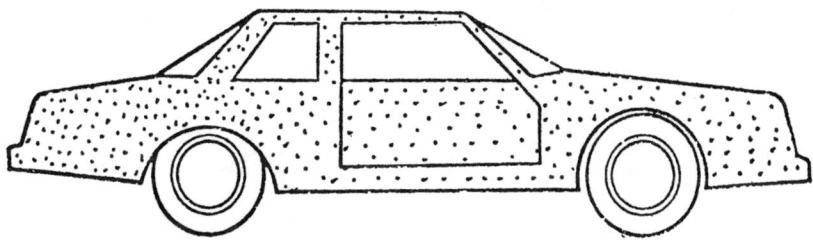

ALL MODELS (1973-1975)

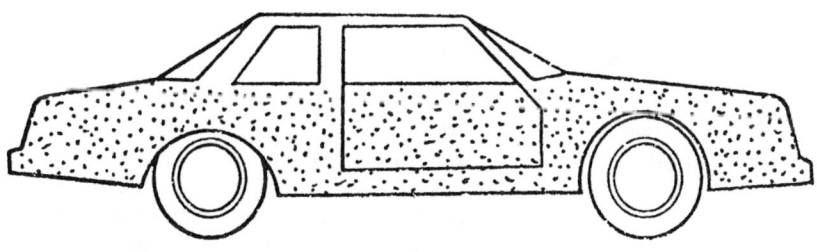

AUSTIN MARINA (1975-1977)

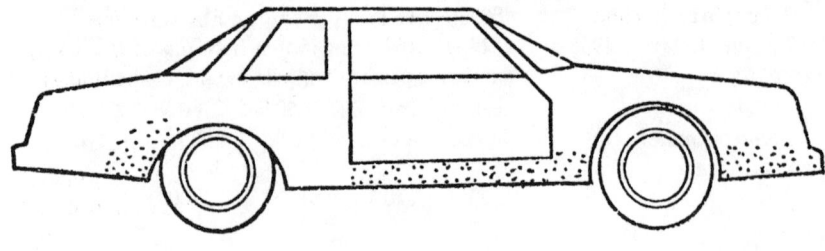

MG (1975–1979)

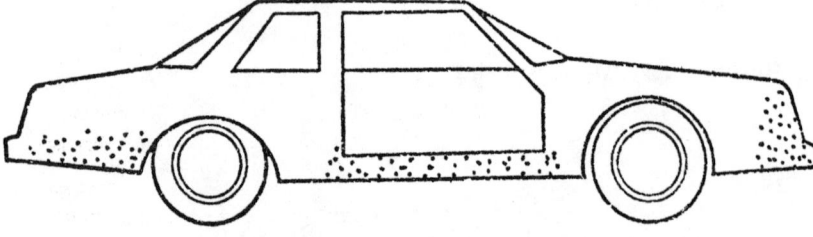

JAGUAR (1975–1979)

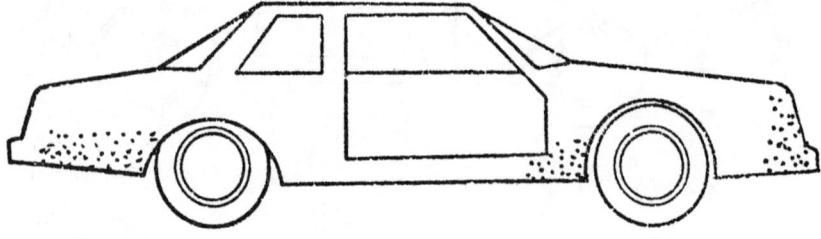

TRIUMPH (1975–1978)

Defect Register

Affected Model
Triumph TR250 and TR6 models from 1968–1976

Defect
Defective lower trunnion pin may shear without warning, causing loss of control. Symptoms of eventual failure include stiff steering and unusually bumpy ride. Pin may break off at low speeds over potholes, or over railroad tracks at high speed.

Affected Model	Defect
Triumph TR250 and TR6 models from 1968–1976	Defective brake proportioning valve may blow its warning switch right out of its socket. Warning light then tells the driver the brakes have failed *after* they have failed.
1977 Triumph TR7 vehicles equipped with optional "Spoker" wheel rims	The "Spoker" wheel is subject to fatigue cracking and possible failure. Failure of the wheel may lead to a loss of vehicle control.
1974–1975 Land Rover	There is a possibility that the front brake flexible hose outer casing may crack and leak brake fluid.
1976 MG Midget	Copper sealing washer situated on the end plug of the brake pressure warning switch may allow slight leakage of brake fluid on brake application reducing braking efficiency.
1976 Triumph TR-7 with V.I.N. range from ACL15278 to ACL29845	Possibility that a few vehicles may have poorly welded rear-axle brackets which support the suspension arms.
1975–1977 Jaguar XJ6 vehicles	There is a possibility of a displacement of the exhaust gas recirculation (E.G.R.) manifold core plugs that could result in engine stalling and loss of power.
1975–1976 Triumph TR7 vehicles	The connection between the accelerator pedal and the throttle control cable can become broken causing a loss of control over engine speed.
1974 Jaguar XJ12s	The tire specification label which is affixed to the glove-compartment door indicates the incorrect tire type in use on the above vehicles.
1974 and 1975 Austin Marina vehicles produced from April 1, 1974, through June 2, 1975	There is a possibility of progressive front flexible brake hose deterioration.
1980 Jaguar XJ6 models	Insufficient clearance between the fuel filter and ignition amplifier may result in fuel leakage and possible engine compartment fire.
1974–1978 Austin Mini	In the event of a rear-end impact, the fuel tank may rupture causing fuel leakage and the possibility of fire.

PEUGEOT

In France, Peugeot is considered the poor man's Citroën. Sophisticated engineering, with economical performance, makes this the perfect car for...France! In North America, the dealer body is too weak and the parts supply too haphazard for the needs of most motorists. Parts prices as well as long waiting periods for repairs have also come in for strong owner criticism.

Of all the Peugeot offerings, owners report that the 304 model gave the best value for its price. Unfortunately, that model has been discontinued, so parts may be a real problem. The newer Peugeot 504 models with diesel engines should be shunned in favor of a good secondhand Mercedes diesel, which sells for the same price.

For those Peugeot owners who have already had diesel motor problems with their 1978 and 1979 Peugeots, free motor repairs can be obtained from the manufacturer under a special "secret" warranty extension.

Industry insiders say that Peugeot has corrected its diesel problems in its 1980–1981 models. If this is true, the only drawbacks to purchasing the Peugeot are its high retail price, sloppy chassis assembly, and biodegradable exhaust system.

Peugeot 504

This model is an example of why some European cars do not sell well in Canada. Regardless of the fact that the Peugeot is well engineered and economical to drive, owners report that service is difficult to find, dealerships may not stay in business very long, parts are difficult to find, parts costs are horrendous, and depreciation is unbelievable. Owners also report problems with the transmission and motor. Models equipped with pollution-control devices have had complaints from owners who find the decrease in road acceleration unacceptable.

Technical Specifications

Peugeot 504:	1976	1977	1978	1979	1980
Wheelbase	108.6"	108"	108"	108"	108.6"
Length	182.8"	182.8"	182.8"	182.4"	182.4"
Width	66.7"	66.7"	66.7"	66.7"	66.7"
Weight	2967 lb.	2900 lb.	3031 lb.	3023 lb.	2948 lb.
Standard motor	4 cyl.	4 cyl.	4 cyl.	4 cyl.	4 cyl.

Peugeot 504:	1976	1977	1978	1979	1980
Gas mileage	19	19	18	18	19
Price	$3300	$4000	$4600	$5500	$7000

Not recommended

Rusting Diagrams for Peugeot

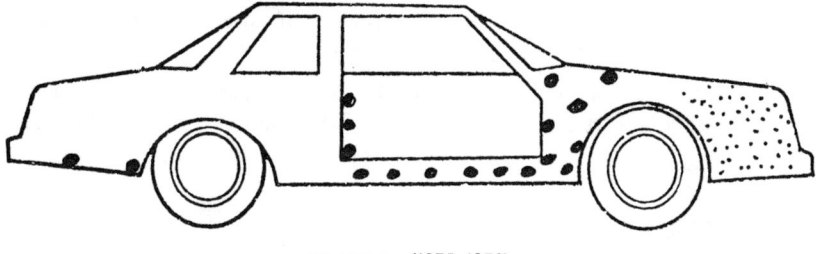

ALL MODELS (1975-1978)

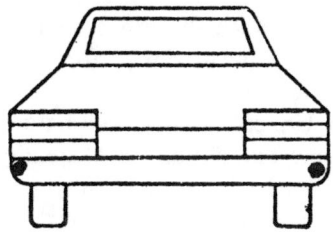
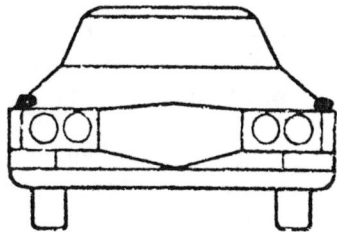

Defect Register

Affected Model
Model 504 and 304 vehicles manufactured between January, 1971, and March, 1974

Defect
Defect on the interior rear view mirror mounting system that contravenes Standard 107.

1975 model 504 diesel sedans and station wagon vehicles

It is possible for the brake lines connecting the dual brake master cylinder to the master brake connector to become corroded from acid emission from the battery and, after some considerable period of time, possibly to cause loss of the brake fluid in one or both of these brake lines.

Affected Model	Defect
Standard and automatic model 504 sedans 1971/72, and cars produced up to January 3, 1973	Rubber windshield moldings on certain vehicles have a hardness level below design specifications and fail to retain, as required by federal law, the windshield, when such vehicles are impacted at 30 MPH into a fixed collision barrier.
Model 304 and 504 vehicles	Back-rest flange could possibly cause abnormal chafing of the safety belt buckle strap under instances of extreme loading, such as during severe vehicle stops.
1977 and 1978 Peugeot 504 Sedan Station Wagon	Possibility that defect exists in brake power booster which could result in reduced braking ability.

RENAULT

Known as the General Motors of France, Renault makes the best engineered, low-priced, economical compact and subcompact vehicles in Europe. Its vehicles maximize both comfort and driving performance while maintaining a solid reputation for fuel economy.

Renault's marketing experience in the United States has been marked by low sales and an inability to find a substantial number of quality dealers capable of servicing its products. As a result of these rather formidable obstacles, the French auto maker practically abandoned the American market in 1965 and concentrated upon its Canadian sales. In retrospect, it was a poor marketing decision prompted by the American motorist's spurning of the defect-prone Renault Dauphine. Renault had the right idea—but the wrong car. Nevertheless, in 1959, it sold 93,000 cars and became the leader in imported-car sales in the United States. This popularity was cut short, however, when other importers, such as Volkswagen, offered better-quality cars at lower prices. Competition got so bad that Renault's total sales in the United States for 1975 were only 7,287 vehicles.

Because of a generally weak dealer network in the United States, parts replacement has always been inadequate and has contributed to the rapid depreciation of Renault models throughout North America. Servicing is another problem area, according to many Renault owners interviewed. Poor diagnostic procedures, mechanical defects that are repaired and then reappear, and difficulty in getting service from independent garages were the major complaints listed. This last problem is a common complaint with many European cars.

Owners report mechanical defects affecting primarily the motor (burning oil and seizing), suspension (front suspension may wear out prematurely from road-spray contaminants), and outer body shell, which is prone to early rusting. Many Renault owners also report they were sold the wrong model year by both new- and used-car dealers. Check the manufacturer's date-of-manufacture plate affixed to the door on the driver's side to determine the true model year.

Although Renault has some very serious problems in servicing its cars, no other auto maker, either European or American, offers such inexpensive, well-engineered vehicles to the North American buying public.

Anyone looking for an excellent used-car buy should carefully consider the Renault 12 which has won a well-deserved reputation for economy and reliability. Although this model's best years were from 1970 through 1972, when pollution-control regulations were less stringent, subsequent model years remain good used-car buys because of their low retail prices caused by a devastatingly rapid depreciation rate. Spare parts are plentiful, since the Renault 12 has had few basic design changes through the years.

Dealer servicing has been a major problem for Renault owners. Renault dealers have not given adequate after-sales service, and owners of the Renault 12 have complained of being overcharged, having to pay for work that should have been done under warranty, of frequent repairs that have not corrected the problem, and arrogant dealers. Nonetheless, the Renault 12 is a solid used-car choice — *if* the price is low and independent servicing is available. Now that Renault has become affiliated with American Motors and servicing will be offered through American Motors dealerships, these service problems should be greatly reduced.

A word of caution—steer clear of the discontinued Renault 16 model. Parts are impossible to find, mechanical defects abound, and even Renault dealers have been known to refuse service on this vehicle. The Renault 16, and also to a lesser extent the Renault 12, has a front-wheel-drive assembly that is failure-prone, owing to its defective "cardan," or rubber protector. Since these failures, which are not safety-related, occur between 24,000 and 36,000 miles, Renault France has secretly extended warranty coverage on these parts and also applied the warranty extension to second owners.

Technical Specifications

Renault 5:	1976	1977	1978	1979	1980
Wheelbase	95.1"	95.1"	95.1"	95.1"	95.2"
Length	142"	142"	142"	142"	142"
Width	60"	60"	60"	60"	60"
Weight	1631 lb.	1683 lb.	1682 lb.	1752 lb.	1792 lb.
Standard motor	4 cyl.	4 cyl.	4 cyl.	4 cyl.	4 cyl.
Gas mileage	26	26	26	26	25
Price	$1700	$2100	$2800	$3600	$5000

Not recommended

Renault 12:	1976	1977	1978	1979
Wheelbase	96"	96"	96"	96"
Length	174"	174"	174"	174"
Width	65"	65"	65"	65"
Weight	2158 lb.	2181 lb.	2183 lb.	2183 lb.
Standard motor	4 cyl.	4 cyl.	4 cyl.	4 cyl.
Gas mileage	26.2	26.1	26	24
Price	$2100	$2500	$3200	$4100

Recommended

Rusting Diagrams for Renault

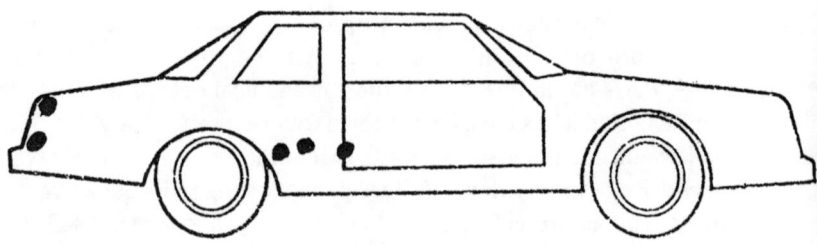

RENAULT 12 (1975–1978)

RENAULT 12 (1970–1975)

Defect Register

Affected Model	*Defect*
1976 Renault 12, 15 and 17 model vehicles within the following serial number ranges: 12 GTL sedan R-1174-9131400 to 9132739 12 STW R-1334-9631000 to 9632330 15 GTL R-1308-7720000 to 7720508 17 GTL R-1328-3793000 to 3793342	If the accelerator linkage primary return spring should become disconnected, the secondary throttle return spring will not exert sufficient force to completely close the throttle within the time limits specified by federal law. Should the defect occur, the driver may have to apply the brakes and/or switch off the ignition to avoid an accident.
1977 Renault 12-TL vehicles, models R-1179 and R-1338 within the following serial number ranges: R-1179 from 9975004 to 9975462 R-1338 from 9620004 to 9620338	The secondary throttle return spring may not exert sufficient force to return the throttle to the idle position within the limits specified by federal law. The driver may have to apply the brakes and/or switch off the ignition to decelerate the vehicle quickly.
1976–1977 Renault 5L vehicles model 1220 with serial number range 6670001 to 6671082	In the event of a disconnection of the primary throttle return spring, the secondary throttle return spring may not exert sufficient force to return the throttle plate to the idle position within the time limits specified by federal law. Drivers may have to apply the brakes and/or switch off the ignition to decelerate the vehicle.
1976 Renault 5 models R1220 with serial number range 6670001 to 6670580 and R1224 with serial number range 7600001 to 7604600	The bonding of the windshield to the body may be defective such that the vehicle will not meet the windshield mounting requirements of federal law.
1976–1977 Renault 5 GTL model R1224 within the serial number range 7600001 to 7606686.	The secondary throttle return spring may not exert sufficient force to return the throttle to the idle position within the time specified by federal law.

Affected Model	Defect
1980 Renault Le Car	Possibility that on certain vehicles, hand brake when fully applied may disengage should downward pressure be applied to top of lever.

BMW

This German company has a fine tradition of quality. Unlike VW, this tradition has not been tarnished by the poor performance of its recent models. In fact, BMW models are excellent used-car buys because of their durability and slow rate of depreciation. Servicing, parts availability, and parts cost can be real problems because the BMW dealership body is very spread out.

BMW designers have given a lot of attention to occupant safety, although they may not advertise the fact as much as Volvo, and this preoccupation can be easily noted with a simple driving test. Visibility is excellent, road handling exceptional, and interior space more than one would expect.

Good reliability, sophisticated engineering, and a slow rate of depreciation combine to make the BMW an expensive and popular dream machine. Owners have complained of inadequate dealer service facilities and many drivers have switched over to independent garages to avoid being stuck with high repair bills. Parts are so scarce and expensive that a black market in used parts presently exists among scrapyards along the northeast coast of the United States.

BMW used-car prices are inflated due to fluctuating European currency rates, the increased retail prices for new models and BMW's well-earned reputation for quality. The best used-car model is the 2002, manufactured before 1976. The 530i six-cylinder model is not recommended, because of early production problems with the fuel-injection system and the problems with finding replacement parts.

BMWs manufactured before 1976 represent the best models of the 2002 series. More recent models in the 530 series are too expensive and have not been on the market in sufficient number to be recommended as good used-car investments. However, models in the 320 series, 1976–1980, are recommended. Be sure that servicing and parts are available before buying any BMW. Also verify the year the car was manufactured. BMW has been a party to one lawsuit for $12,000 where an owner proved a BMW dealer sold a new BMW for the wrong model year.

Technical Specifications

BMW 320i:	1976	1977	1978	1979	1980
Wheelbase	98.4"	100.9"	100.9"	100.9"	100.9"
Length	176"	177.5"	177.5"	177.5"	177.5"
Width	62.6"	63"	63"	63"	63.4"
Weight	2860 lb.	2646 lb.	2430 lb.	2358 lb.	2446 lb.
Standard motor	4 cyl.	4 cyl.	4 cyl.	4 cyl.	4 cyl.
Gas mileage	27	25	25	26	25
Price	$4500	$5600	$6500	$8000	$9000

Recommended

Rusting Diagram for BMW

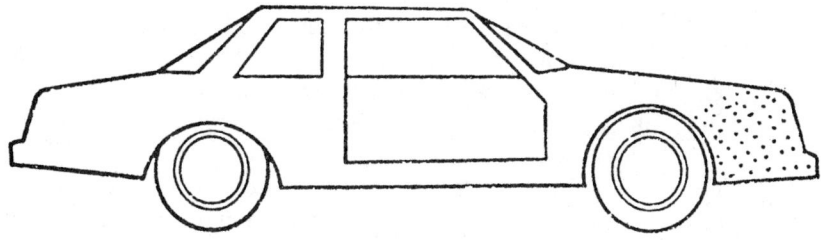

ALL MODELS (1972-1976)

Defect Register

Affected Model
1973-1974 Bavaria /3.OS, 1973-1974 3.OCS, 1975-1977 530i, 1975-1976 3.OSi and 1977 630 CSi vehicles equipped with power windows

Defect
The power window system on the subject vehicles does not fully comply with federal laws.

1977 BMW 320i automobiles within the following serial number ranges:
320i 5420001 to 5429194
320i automatic 5470001 to 5473124

Two engine mounted throttle return springs may oscillate and break. If the throttle return spring breaks, the accelerator may not return to the idle position as required by federal law.

Affected Model	Defect
1977–1978 BMW 320i vehicles built from September, 1976, to December, 1977	Periods of extreme cold temperatures can cause the rubber protective dirt sleeve on the throttle cable to become stiff, preventing the throttle from returning to the idle position as required by federal law. Operators may have to apply the brakes and/or switch off the ignition to decelerate the vehicle quickly.
1979 BMW 320i and 320iA	Possibility that electrically operated fuel pump which is installed in fuel tank may have wiring connectors on fuel pump assembly that are loose and can result in interruption of current flow.

MERCEDES-BENZ

Although no larger than an intermediate-sized car, Mercedes-Benz models offer buyers luxury that is often left out of similar high-priced models. New models are expensive, but depreciation is very slow, and with the inflation of the American economy, Mercedes-Benz models lose very little of their value as they age.

Owners report that parts availability and dealer servicing is good, possibly as a result of the popularity of the car and the demands made by some of the more affluent Mercedes owners. Dealers have a quasi-monopoly over parts and may abuse their position to charge artificially inflated prices. Most used Mercedes-Benz models can be repaired by independent garages specializing in European cars or truck mechanics experienced in repairing diesel engines.

Diesel models seem to have the best frequency of repair records and are the best used-car buy. They are noisy, however. Fuel for these models may also freeze at low temperatures and cause engine malfunctioning. (Mercedes-Benz is working on an additive to correct this problem.) Other Mercedes models are also good buys. Make sure, though, that the car is of the right model year.

Some owners have complained of the premature rusting of their Mercedes-Benz exhaust system; however, some dealers have admitted that this problem has been covered by an extended warranty from the manufacturer as long as the rusting occurs within the first two years of ownership. Mercedes-Benz has kept quiet about this special warranty policy, so there is still no official confirmation that it exists.

Mercedes owners have also given some negative reports concerning the frequent replacement of the exhaust system in colder climates, and the charges for periodic maintenance work. Some customers have reported that Mercedes will pay 50 percent of the bill for the replacement of the exhaust system within the first two years of ownership. This alleged warranty extension, like the one concerning rusting, has not been confirmed.

During the past few years, owners report an increasing number of quality-control problems that cut down the reliability of the Mercedes. Most of these complaints concern the brakes and carburetor. Because of the nature of these complaints it's hard to determine whether they are indicative of poor factory quality control or incompetent service at the dealership level. After-sales service by Mercedes-Benz dealers has not been all that impressive.

Technical Specifications

Mercedes-Benz 220D and 240D:	1976	1977	1978	1979	1980
Wheelbase	108.3"	108.3"	108.3"	108.3"	110"
Length	195"	190"	190"	190"	190"
Width	—	—	—	—	69.7"
Weight	3041 lb.	3041 lb.	3110 lb.	3080 lb.	3205 lb.
Standard motor	4 cyl.	4 cyl.	4 cyl.	4 cyl.	4 cyl.
Gas mileage	22.7	23.4	23.1	24.1	24.3
Price	$2700	$4000	$5000	$6500	$7500

Recommended

Rusting Diagram For Mercedes-Benz

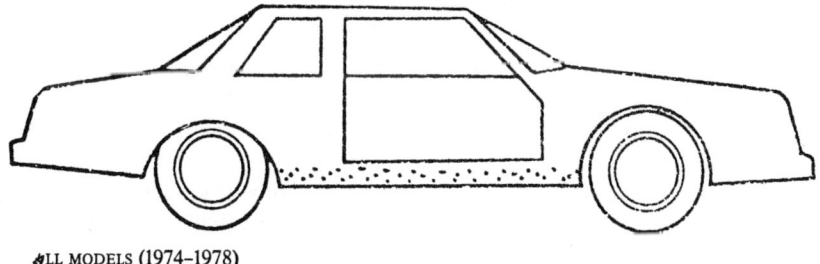

ALL MODELS (1974–1978)

Defect Register

Affected Model
1976 Models 280, 280C, 280S, 300D, 450SE, 450SEL, 450SL and 450SLC passenger cars

Defect
The Cruise Control Bowden Cable may bind.

1973–1975 Mercedes-Benz 450 SL and 450 SLC models equipped with cruise control

The cruise control actuator located on the wheel well is subject to excessive corrosion and therefore will be relocated. There is a possibility that corrosion could cause the cruise control mechanism to fail to operate as desired.

1978–1979 Mercedes Benz 3005D

Possibility that crankshaft pulley could separate from mounting plate due to manufacturing defect.

VOLKSWAGEN

Audi

The Audi is a Volkswagen model that has tarnished the rising VW star. Owners complain of major mechanical defects such as an exhaust system that self-destructs and premature brake wear around 10,000 miles. The motor often acts like an old-fashioned oil burner, and reports from Audi owners of major engine overhauls between 24,000 and 36,000 miles are not uncommon. The transmission may also malfunction because of defective internal gears. Much to its credit, Volkswagen has extended the warranty coverage on the exhaust system, motor, and transmission defects up to 36,000 miles.

Many Audi owners report that servicing is expensive and parts are constantly on back order. Consequently, many owners polled stated they would not buy another Audi.

Since 1980, the Audi 5000 model has brought back some of the customers the company lost through the poor quality of its early Audi models. There has already been a reduction in consumer complaints from Audi owners who have purchased the 1978 and 1979 models. If Volkswagen does continue to improve the car, it should sell quite well. However, before recommending the purchase of a used Audi, more information from the owners of the 1978, 1979, and 1980 models will be necessary.

Technical Specifications

Audi Fox/Audi 4000:	1976	1977	1978	1979
Wheelbase	97.2"	97.2"	96.5"	98.2"
Length	172"	172"	172"	172"
Width	64.7"	64"	64"	64"
Weight	2000 lb.	2030 lb.	2070 lb.	2030 lb.
Standard motor	4 cyl.	4 cyl.	4 cyl.	4 cyl.
Gas mileage	27	28	27	27
Price	$2000	$2500	$3100	$4000

Not recommended

Rusting Diagram for Audi

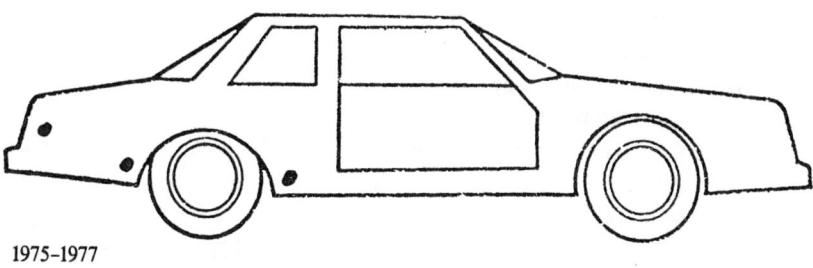

1975-1977

Defect Register

Affected Model
1975 Audi 100 models, equipped with automatic transmission, with chassis numbers ranges: 815 100 5871 to 815 102 5687

Defect
The securing nut which holds the front exhaust pipe support bracket to the transmission housing can become loose and eventually fall off. Consequently, the exhaust pipe support bracket may vibrate, contact, and eventually damage the return fuel lines.

1981 Audi 4000

The interior surface of the threaded hole for the front brake caliper brake hoses may contain porous spots which would allow brake fluid to seep out of the calipers during heavy brake applications.

Beetle/Rabbit

The Beetle had always been Volkswagen's ideal city car, with a solid reputation for economy, reliability, and defective heaters that almost never worked in the winter. Unfortunately, America's love affair with the VW came to a sad and untimely end when the company phased out the Beetle in the mid-1970's. Japanese and other European models are now taking an increasingly larger share of the imported-car market.

Since Volkswagen abandoned the Beetle, it has repeatedly struck out with its subsequent models. The Audi, Dasher, VW 411 and 412 have all been losers, and Volkswagen seemed to be intent on continuing that tradition with its 1975–1976 Rabbit and Scirocco models.

These Rabbit owners reported chronic starting problems, inoperative door locks, defective interior trim and finish, body rattles, transmission clunks, and exhaust-system thumps. Rubber dampers used to protect the exhaust system from striking the chassis also had a high failure rate. In addition to serious mechanical defects, Rabbit and Scirocco owners also said that dealer service was expensive and spare parts scarce. Fires have been reported in Volkswagens in California, owing to a defective catalytic-converter system. This model has since been recalled.

Because of Volkswagen's serious shortcomings with its Rabbit/Scirocco models, the company has extended the warranty on its 1975 models to "upgrade the 1975's to the level of the 1976's," according to Josef L. Metz, vice president in charge of corporate service, Volkswagen of America. Rabbit/Scirocco owners received free repairs for problems in the following areas: brakes, poor driveability, carburetor malfunctioning, exhaust system rattles, cold-starting difficulties, and plastic door trim defects. This major warranty extension program cost VW more than $5 million and could possibly affect more than 100,000 vehicles.

In an analysis of Rabbit-owner complaints concerning 1977–1979 Rabbit models, the Automotive Protection Association has discovered serious allegations of safety-related and performance-related defects.

Safety-Related Problems

1. Brake master cylinder. Owners of 1976 and 1977 Rabbits, Dashers, Sciroccos, and Audi Foxes may experience sudden failure of the braking system due to a defective master cylinder.

2. Sudden engine surge. Motorists report that 1978 diesel models may suddenly surge ahead during highway driving. This unexpected acceleration may last 10-15 seconds and make the vehicle practically uncontrollable.

3. Catastrophic motor seizure. More than 80 percent of the Rabbit owners surveyed complained of engine failures that often were extensive and expensive to repair. In most cases it was the cylinder head that had to be replaced. Repair bills ranging from $1500 to $2000 were not uncommon. Both diesel and gasoline Rabbit engines were equally failure-prone.

4. Exploding oil filters. Some Rabbit owners reported that their oil filters exploded or cracked without any prior warning. In one case, a driver found that excessive engine oil pressure blew off the oil filter cap of his 1978 diesel Rabbit. Another owner had to replace three oil filters and pay for major engine repairs on his 1979 diesel Rabbit because the oil filter cracked and the oil filter gasket malfunctioned.

Performance-Related Problems

Only the complaints of owners of 1977-1979 Rabbits were considered in the tabulation of these problem areas. Earlier models showed an even worse frequency-of-repair history. Problems are listed according to their severity and how frequently they were reported.

Diesel Rabbit.
1. Cylinder head replacement
2. Complete engine failure
3. Glow plugs
4. Oil leaks
5. Defective injectors
6. Exploding oil filters
7. Defective oil filter gaskets
8. Brake noise
9. Generator-oil pump fan belt failures
10. Crankshaft pully breakage
11. "Fuel contamination"
12. Fuel pump
13. Heater
14. Poor starting (humidity)

Gasoline Rabbit.
1. Complete motor replacement
2. Alternator failures
3. Cylinder head replacement
4. Cylinder head replacement (12-24 months)
5. Fuse box corrosion
6. Fuel distributor
7. Engine transmission vibrations
8. Hard starting (hot and cold)

9. Sudden loss of engine oil
10. Fuel injectors
11. Electrical malfunctions (lights, horn, wipers, gauges)
12. Heater malfunctions
13. Window hinges unglued
14. Stalling
15. Fuse box relay
16. Fuel gauge
17. Brakes (premature wear)
18. Noisy brakes
19. Hard shifting

Service-Related Problems
1. Spare parts unavailable
2. High parts and labor costs
3. Dealer servicing unavailable
4. Extensive repairs performed on minor problems
5. Engine failures blamed upon owner negligence without complete investigation
6. Courtesy car unavailable

Technical Specifications

VW Beetle:	1970	1971	1972	1973	1974	1975
Wheelbase	94.5"	—	—	—	—	94.5"
Length	160.6"	—	—	—	—	163.4"
Width	—	—	—	—	—	61"
Weight	1675 lb.	1807 lb.	—	1764 lb.	1764 lb.	1896 lb.
Standard motor	4 cyl.	4 cyl.	4 cyl.	4 cyl.	4 cyl.	4 cyl.
Gas mileage	29.3	27.5	27.9	27.3	29.1	29.4
Price	$800	$1000	$1200	$1500	$1900	$2700

Recommended

VW Rabbit:	1975	1976	1977	1978	1979	1980
Wheelbase	94.5"	94.5"	94.5"	94.5"	96"	94.4"
Length	155.3"	155.3"	155.3"	155.3"	155.3"	155.3"
Width	63.4"	63.4"	63.4"	63.4"	63.4"	63.4"
Weight	1830 lb.	1830 lb.	1840 lb.	1840 lb.	1850 lb.	1850 lb.
Standard motor	4 cyl.	4 cyl.	4 cyl.	4 cyl.	4 cyl.	4 cyl.
Gas mileage	26	28	29	34	37	40
Price	$2800	$3000	$4000	$4700	$5500	$6300

Not recommended

Rusting Diagrams for Volkswagen Rabbit

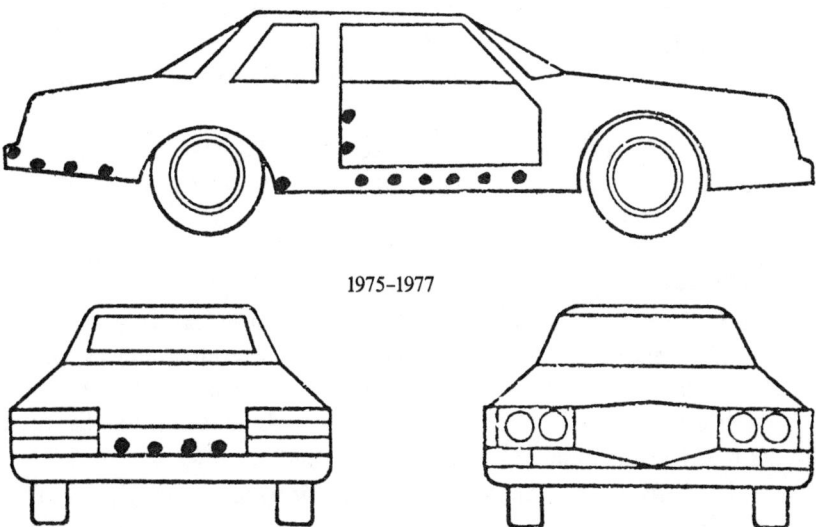

1975–1977

Defect Register

Affected Model
1978 Rabbit and Scirocco vehicles within the serial number ranges:
Rabbit 1783000001 to 1783113228
Scirocco 5382000001 to 5382017510

Defect
Two rubber elbow connections located at each end of the plastic pipe leading from the throttle valve body housing to the brake booster vacuum pump may have been damaged by the installation of improper clamps. Damaged connections could cause engine stalling and/or insufficient brake booster vacuum which would require the use of greater brake pedal pressure and longer stopping distances.

1975 Type 1 Volkswagen vehicles manufactured from August to October, 1974

Defect involves loose hose clamps due to assembly shortcomings. The clamps are used to hold the injector hose for each cylinder to the fuel feed lines. Routine new vehicle quality control check revealed fuel leakage on some of the hoses described.

Porsche

The ideal medium-priced sports car. While giving excellent overall driving performance and fuel economy, Porsche also brings with it a strong dealer network and a good supply of replacement parts. Depreciation is less than average, helping to offset the initial high retail-sales price.

Porsche owners have complained that dealer servicing is expensive, so it may be a good idea to cut loose from the dealer servicing as soon as the warranty period is terminated.

The mid-engined 914 is a much better buy as a used-car investment than the rear-engined 911, because the 914 can be bought used for almost half the price of a used 911. The 914 is also a more forgiving car on the highway and does not require as much of the expert handling as the 911. Don't look for used-car bargains, though; Porsche owners are usually well informed about their car's value and will not sell below list price unless there is some costly mechanical repair on the horizon.

The demand for the 911 models exceeds by far the supply. Even the 928 and 924 models cannot keep pace with the overwhelming popularity of the 911. If this trend continues the 928 and 924 models will depreciate more quickly and become more realistically priced used cars in much the same way as the 914 model.

Technical Specifications

Porsche 911:	*1975*	*1976*	*1977*	*1978*	*1979*	*1980*
Wheelbase	89.4"	89.4"	89.5"	89.5"	89.5"	89.5"
Length	168.9"	168.9"	169"	169"	169"	168.9"
Width	63.3"	63.3"	63.3"	63.3"	63.3"	63.3"
Weight	2425 lb.	2425 lb.	2560 lb.	2560 lb.	2560 lb.	2650 lb.
Standard motor	6 cyl.	6 cyl.	6 cyl.	6 cyl.	6 cyl.	6 cyl.
Gas mileage	25.7	21	20	17	17	16
Price	$11,000	$12,000	$14,500	$17,000	$20,000	$23,000

Recommended

Defect Register

Affected Model	*Defect*
1976–1978 Porsche 911 vehicles equipped with automatic speed control	The vehicles do not have instructions regarding the speed control unit attached to or adjacent to the unit as required by federal law.
1970–1975 Porsche 914 model vehicles equipped with four-cylinder engines	It is possible that rain or car wash water could settle on top of the battery, if the battery cover is missing, damaged, or improperly installed, and form an acid solution which may damage nearby fuel hoses. The damaged hoses may leak gasoline and cause an engine compartment fire.
1974–1975 model Porsche 911 passenger cars	Due to inductive interference between the ignition cables, backfiring may occur. This could result in damage to the mixture control unit to the extent of rendering the vehicle inoperative and the possibility of fire.
1978 Porsche 928	Possibility that front axle caster and camber adjusters could crack as a result of improper hardening during production.

ALFA ROMEO

In 1973, the suggested retail price of the Alfa Romeo Berlina was $5110. Four years later, many of the same 1973 Berlina models were selling for as much as $2500 on the used-car market. This is the most striking example of the Alfa Romeo's ability to maintain a high resale value despite its relatively high price when bought new. The slow depreciation and popularity of the Alfa models contrasts greatly with the rapid depreciation and consumer disdain found with most other European cars.

People like Alfa Romeo cars mainly for their European sports-car performance. Sensitive steering, advanced suspension systems, radial tires, high-performance engines, and good brakes provide Alfa owners with the feeling of absolute control over their vehicles.

Alfa Romeos are serviced by an inadequate network of Fiat dealers.

Parts are often in short supply and repair charges may be expensive. Many Alfa owners steer clear of the dealer network, preferring independent garages that specialize in the repair of European cars.

When buying a used Alfa, verify the true model year by checking the date the car was manufactured. One Fiat dealer has been found guilty of falsifying model years on Fiats, so caution is in order when buying the popular Alfa from a used-car dealer or private seller. A mechanical inspection by an independent garage is also necessary, since Alfa Romeos are fragile cars that fall into disrepair quickly if not well-maintained.

Alfa owners have complained that their cars do not respond well to climatic extremes. A free cold-starting carburetor kit has been supplied by the manufacturer to owners of 1971–1973 Berlinas. This warranty extension has not been generally publicized by the manufacturer.

The Alfa is a fair-weather sports car, highly recommended for mild weather zones like California, Florida, and other areas south of latitude 40. The initial retail price is high and depreciation is low despite the small dealer network. The Berlina Sedan, Spider Veloce, and GTV 2 plus 2 Coupe are excellent used-car buys.

With fuel injection, dual overhead cam, a two-liter engine, five-speed transmission and four-wheel disc brakes as standard equipment, the Alfa needs few options. A well-maintained Alfa Romeo is a joy to behold (and to drive).

Owners of Alfa Romeo models built after 1977 report an improvement in starting and dealership servicing.

Technical Specifications

Sedan 2000:	1976	1977	1978	1979	1980
Wheelbase	98.8"	98.8"	98.8"	97.8"	97.8"
Length	172.5"	172"	172"	172"	172"
Width	63.8"	63"	63"	63"	63"
Weight	2690 lb.	2690 lb.	2690 lb.	2690 lb.	2853 lb.
Standard motor	4 cyl.	4 cyl.	4 cyl.	4 cyl.	4 cyl.
Gas mileage	23.1	21	21	21	20
Price	$5500	$6400	$7600	$9500	$11,000

Recommended

Rusting Diagrams for Alfa Romeo

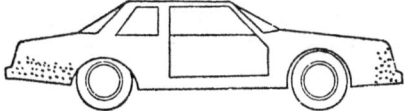 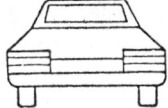 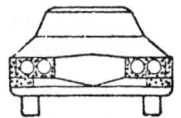

1975-1979

Defect Register

Affected Model
All 1975 and 1976 Alfa Romeo Alfetta Sedans and Alfetta GT models produced with Klippan front seat belts up to the following chassis numbers: Alfetta Sedan 116.33.000.3322 Alfetta FT 116.29.000.3118, and some 267 Alfetta Sedans and 252 Alfetta GT models. Vehicles with seat-belt assemblies manufactured by Irvin are not affected.

Defect
The safety seat belt retracting mechanism may not lock up the shoulder harness as intended.

1976 and 1977 Alfetta 11615, 11629, 11633, 11634

Possibility that under severe use "high hysteresis" rear rubber coupling of drive shaft may develop fatigue cracks with resulting transmission vibration.

FIAT

Fiat 124/Fiat 128

Since the 124 model was first launched in 1968, Fiat's reputation has been a series of up and downs, but the downs seem to far outnumber the ups. The introduction of Fiat's 128 model in 1972 did little to enhance the Fiat image in America. Both of these models tend to rust after only a few years of use. This premature rusting has been known to pose a safety hazard since the suspension components that are attached to the chassis may come loose and make the car uncontrollable. Fiat 128 models are especially vulnerable in 1971–1973 model years. Fiats have rapid depreciation, parts shortages, inadequate dealer network, and high service charges.

Obviously, both the 124 and 128 models have been well designed — for Italy. In America, however, the climate, poor dealer and parts availability, and the competition of other, more robust models have contributed to Fiat's cool reception. Owners report problems with the motor, body, and exhaust system of both the 124 and 128 models. Others have said they were sold the wrong model year by their dealer. Until Fiat creates a stronger parts-distribution system and constructs its vehicles to withstand the rigors of harsh climates, none of its used cars are a safe investment.

Fiats are freaky. They are well-built machines that have given millions of European motorists excellent fuel economy while providing sports-car performance on the highway. American motorists should expect the same, but according to the hundreds of complaint letters pouring into American auto consumer groups, such as the Washington Center for Auto Safety, Fiat imports take on a classic Dr. Jekyll and Mr. Hyde disposition as they cross the Atlantic.

Owners are most concerned over what they call inadequate servicing. Complaints regarding the high cost of parts replacement and periodic maintenance abound. And because of the poor after-sales service by Fiat's weak dealer body, many Fiat owners state they would never buy another one.

Reliability is another problem area reported by Fiat owners that could be traced back to poor service procedures. Although owners reported their cars gave excellent gas mileage, many complained of frequent stalling or surging that was difficult to correct at the dealer level. Cold-weather performance north of the fortieth parallel also was said to be unacceptable.

By far the most angry responses from Fiat owners came from those who were asked about Fiat's warranty performance. They complained that Fiat dealers would often overcharge for periodic inspections, charge for warranty work that was supposed to be free, or stall warranty work until the warranty period elapsed and then "discover" that the work was urgent. Just so Fiat will not feel this criticism is unfair, they are invited to read the numerous small-claims-court decisions on file, which back up each of the above allegations. Fiat officials in the United States have promised to reform their warranty procedures. However, judging by the complaints still being received, this promise is not very convincing.

Fiat's Biodegradable Body

One of the main reasons why most Fiat models are a terrible new- or used-car choice is the rapid and almost total deterioration of the chassis by premature rusting.

Fiat owners in England, France, Germany, and Sweden, have been particularly victimized by the severe chassis corrosion of Fiats 850, 124, 126, 127, and 128 models manufactured between 1969 and 1976.

The American government has sued Fiat for $1.6 million for failing to adequately recall and buy back rusting 1970–1971 Fiat 850 models. The government also has sued Fiat to recall 133,500 of its 1970–1974 Fiat 124 models for the same defect: premature corrosion that weakens the vehicle's undercarriage, steering, and suspension components.

Prior to the American lawsuit, Fiat had promised to buy back for $600 every rusty vehicle with less than 70,000 miles. Government investigations charge, however, that Fiat broke this promise and used "coercive tactics" to persuade owners to accept inadequate compensation.

The major mechanical defects complained of by Fiat owners run the gamut of every possibility. European owners report that Fiat models have a generally worse than average reputation for breakdowns. Older models are reported to have motor, clutch, and suspension problems, while those cars made during the past three years manifest troublesome ignition systems and an inadequate brake performance.

Fiat's hard times with its 1979 and 1980 models have been caused primarily by its weak dealer network of only 700 American dealers, many of whom have dual dealerships. These dealers are often tempted to make up their low sales profits through high service charges in their repair bills.

So, although Fiat has improved its product, Fiat dealers must still put up with low profits and an erratic parts delivery system. The company also lost 200,000 units in 1979 because of strikes.

Owners of 1976–1980 Fiats report problems with the suspension, motor, and coachwork. Rusting, however, no longer appears to be a problem. Fiat's warranty of performance has been below average, probably due to the company's tight-fisted attitude in dealing with consumer complaints.

Following Nissan Datsun's lead, Fiat has agreed to pay dealers the regular retail repair rate for warranty repairs. This new warranty reimbursement program will give Fiat dealers more money to carry out warranty repairs under Fiat's 24-month/24,000 mile warranty. In the past, Fiat dealers often put a low priority on warranty repairs because of inadequate compensation from Fiat.

Fiat Sports Cars and Sedans

Fiat has two sports cars, the X1/9 and the Spider 2000, that have proved popular despite their transmission and motor problems. These models retain well their resale value and are a big hit with sports-car enthusiasts who really know very little about sports cars.

The Strada and Brava sedan models were introduced in 1979 to compete toe-to-toe with the VW Rabbit and BMW. The Strada is priced low enough to compete favorably with the Volkswagen Rabbit. But while projections for the current year show imports making record gains (21 percent of the American market) Fiat officials admit that these gains, estimated at two million new cars, will mostly benefit Japanese automakers.

Technical Specifications

Fiat 131 (Brava):	1976	1977	1978	1979	1980
Wheelbase	98"	98"	98"	98"	98"
Length	172.4"	172.4"	172.4"	172.4"	172.4"
Width	66.7"	65"	65"	65"	65"
Weight	2455 lb.	2455 lb.	2430 lb.	2490 lb.	2550 lb.
Standard motor	4 cyl.	4 cyl.	4 cyl.	4 cyl.	4 cyl.
Gas mileage	26	25	25	24	26
Price	$2800	$3700	$4400	$5800	$6500

Not recommended

Fiat 128:	1976	1977	1978	1979
Wheelbase	96.4"	96.4"	96.4"	96.4"
Length	158.6"	158"	158"	158"
Width	62"	62"	62"	62"
Weight	2005 lb.	1990 lb.	1975 lb.	1950 lb.
Standard motor	4 cyl.	4 cyl.	4 cyl.	4 cyl.
Gas mileage	28	27	27	26.5
Price	$1200	$1700	$2500	$3500

Not recommended

Rusting Diagrams for Fiat

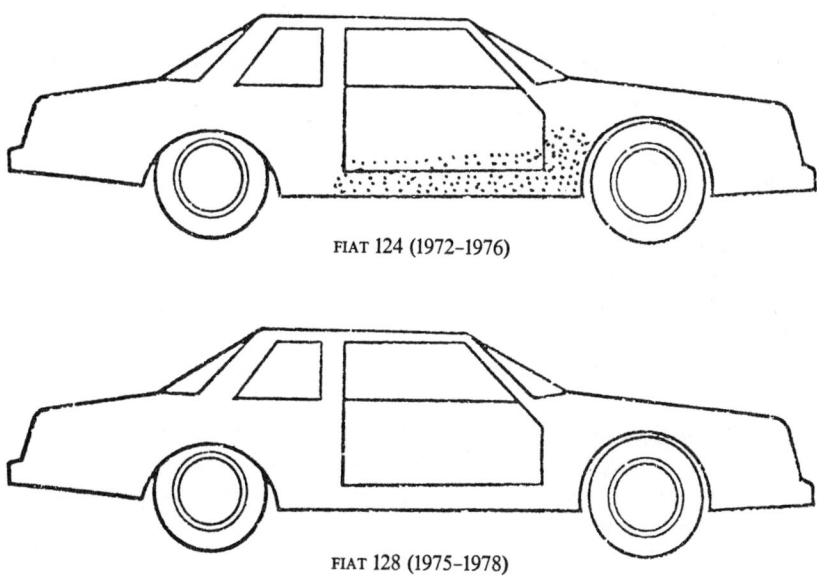

FIAT 124 (1972-1976)

FIAT 128 (1975-1978)

Defect Register

Affected Model

1975-1976 Fiat 131 models with standard transmission. Two- and four-door models have a serial number range to 220951

1975-1976 Fiat 131 within the following serial numbers:
Sedan 000001 to 265524
Station wagon 4000001 to 4097359

1974 and 1975 Fiat X 1/9 passenger cars produced from September, 1973, to September, 1975

Defect

Operation of the vehicle for extended periods at highway speeds could cause the rear transmission bushing to fail, with the possibility of vehicle crash.

Premature wear of the rear rubber seal of the brake master cylinder will allow abnormal air infiltration into the hydraulic system and cause progressively longer brake pedal travel. Although the rear braking system will not be affected, the braking capacity of the vehicle will be impaired and may lead to a vehicle crash.

There is a possibility that the accelerator cable was installed in a manner which could cause the accelerator assembly to function abnormally.

Affected Model	Defect
1975 Beta Sedan built from March, 1975, to October, 1975 1977 Beta Sedan built from July, 1976, to August, 1976 1975 Beta Coupe built from March, 1975, to August, 1975 1976 Beta Coupe built from July, 1975, to August, 1976 1977 HPE built from July, 1976, to August, 1976	Brackets connecting the front suspension arms to the supporting subframe may not have been completely welded to the subframe. If the brackets separate vehicle handling will be impaired with the possibility of a vehicle crash without prior warning to the driver.
1975 Lancia Beta Sedan (500001–502504), 1975 Lancia Beta Coupe (500001–500493 and 600494–602005)	The brakeline from the master cylinder to the left front brake may have been installed in such a way as to come into contact with the clutch cable housing.
1979 Fiat Strada	Possibility that tail lights may become inoperative due to oxidation of tail light and wiring terminals caused by water and dirt infiltration.
1980 Fiat X1/9	Possibility that on certain vehicles outside rearview mirror on driver's side may lack proper magnification in that objects viewed may appear farther away than their actual distance.

DATSUN

Until it introduced the 1974 model year, Datsun had an excellent reputation for building inexpensive subcompacts that gave excellent fuel economy and provided plenty of space for passengers. This reputation was made by the Datsun 1600 (510) and the 1200 models during their model year run from 1967 to 1973. Of course these models had their defects like malfunctioning coils, a weak suspension, and premature self-destruction of the muffler (Datsun extended the warranty on this problem).

After making its reputation with very economical and efficient small cars like the 510, Datsun has now contracted "Detroit fever" by adding on a lot of unnecessary gimmick options that price its cars out of reach for many economy-minded motorists. All of Datsun's early 510 models, especially the two-door 1973 model, are highly recommended, despite premature rusting, electrical and tire defects.

The 1971 and 1972 Datsun 240Z had very serious brake defects for which the vehicle was never recalled.

Rusting has been so bad on the 240Z, B210 and the 510 that Datsun has bought back, through its dealers, some vehicles in which premature rusting had weakened the frames.

Ever since Datsun stopped making its highly successful 510 series in 1973, the company's fortunes have been going steadily downhill. The only Datsun models that have proved successful during the past seven years have been the "Z" cars.

The compact B210, introduced in 1974, has been a dismal failure beset by insufficient interior space and severe premature chassis rusting. The rusting problem has been so bad that Datsun attempted to buy back many of its B210 models rendered unsafe by the deterioration of its front suspension. In 1979, Datsun introduced a six-year rust warranty.

In February, 1977, Datsun introduced its new 200-SX model to fill the gap between the mid-range models and the more expensive "Z" cars. Unfortunately, the public spurned Datsun's new model and only 70,000 units were sold in its first three years. Base price for the 1981 200-SX is $6900, which is about $800 cheaper than the new remodeled 510 model. Neither of these two models is recommended, either new or used.

Datsun's 610 model is no winner, either. It is an overweight, overstyled vehicle that gives poor fuel economy and depreciates rapidly.

Datsun's new 210 model, with a 1.2-liter engine and four-speed transmission promises to take up the slack left by the discontinued 1200 series.

Datsun has also had trouble with its front-wheel drive models. The front-wheel drive F10 model, introduced in 1978, has been plagued by poor quality control and unreliable performance ever since. The new 310 front-wheel-drive model, however, is a much better new- or used-car buy.

Sports-car fans will be pleased with Datsun's restyling of the "Z" sports cars, begun in 1979 with the 280-ZX. The 1981 models have improved seating, redesigned hatch roof, and a refined air-conditioning system.

Datsun's pickup trucks are the only bright spot in its used-car line-up. Their low initial cost, durability, and reliability make them a good choice for anyone looking for a good used vehicle.

Aside from the pickup trucks, the best used-car buys for Datsun shoppers are the 510, 1200, and station wagon models. Every model should be carefully inspected for rust damage before its purchase.

Technical Specifications

Datsun B210:	1976	1977	1978	1979	1980
Wheelbase	92.1"	92"	92"	92.1"	92.1"
Length	160"	160"	160"	160"	165"
Width	60.6"	60"	60"	60"	62.2"
Weight	2095 lb.	1864 lb.	1864 lb.	1990 lb.	1900 lb.
Standard motor	4 cyl.	4 cyl.	4 cyl.	4 cyl.	4 cyl.
Gas mileage	30	29	29	28	30
Price	$1400	$1900	$2300	$3200	$4200

Not recommended

Datsun "Z" cars:	1976	1977	1978	1979	1980
Wheelbase	90.7"	91"	98.6"	98.4"	91.3"
Length	173.2"	173"	174"	174"	174"
Width	64.2"	64"	66"	66"	66"
Weight	2765 lb.	2628 lb.	2628 lb.	2628 lb.	2786 lb.
Standard motor	6 cyl.	6 cyl.	6 cyl.	6 cyl.	6 cyl.
Gas mileage	23	22	22	20	18
Price	$3500	$5000	$6500	$7900	$8800

Recommended

Rusting Diagrams for Datsun

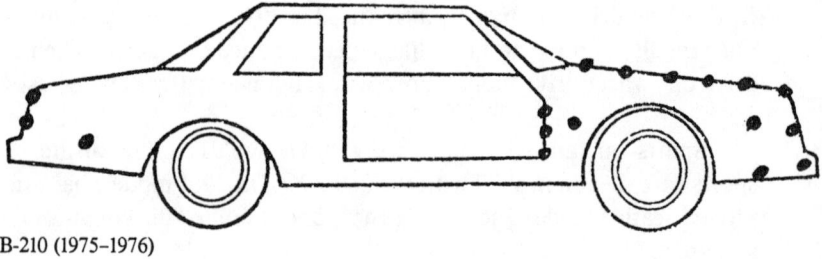

B-210 (1975–1976)

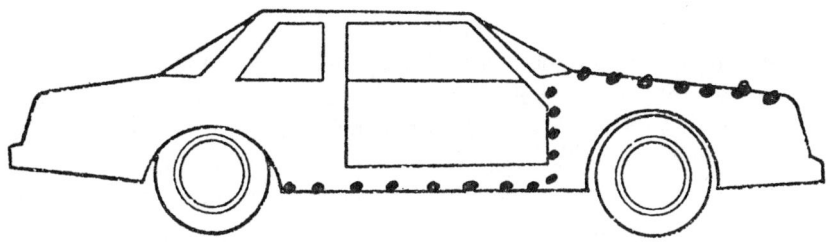

240Z/260Z (1971–1975)

Defect Register

Affected Model	*Defect*
1975 Datsun 280Z built between December, 1974, and August, 1975, with VIN range HLS30-200001 to 225319 GHLS30-000001 to 007045	Engine compartment fuel line hose clamp tends to deform when being tightened, allowing fuel seepage into the engine compartment with danger of fire.
1980 Datsun 310	Possibility that on certain vehicles main shaft lock nut can come loose due to incorrect torquing operation during assembly. This can lead to difficulties in shifting.

HONDA

When Honda first launched its front-wheel drive economy cars in 1975, they became an instant success due to their low retail price, excellent fuel economy, and liberal warranty guidelines.

Unfortunately, just 6 years later, a flood of Honda owner complaint letters received by government consumer protection agencies and private consumer groups show that, in many instances, Honda's "economy" car is a defect-ridden, unreliable, and a potentially deadly small car.

In 1978, the Automobile Protection Association opened a special dossier on safety-related and performance-related defects reported by hundreds of Honda owners with additional information from confidential Honda documents, interviews with Honda dealers, and meetings with former employees.

"Small" Problems Getting Bigger

For years, Honda owners have complained of motor, body, and brake problems. These defects did not affect Honda's sales, though, due to the company's wise policy of compensating owners long after the warranty period had expired. This fair and effective corporate policy was instrumental in maintaining owner loyalty, avoiding confrontation with consumer protection agencies, and fostering the false impression that Honda cars were better built vehicles than the competition.

This masquerade was successful until late 1977, when warranty compensation funds seemingly dried up and owner complaints dramatically increased. These complaints showed patterns of mechanical breakdowns and paint/rust problems that indicated the presence of serious design deficiencies. It was obvious that many of the defects reported in the past as "minor", were really major problems experienced by hundreds, possibly thousands, of other Honda owners.

A Deluge of Defects 1975-1979

Although, not all Hondas have the same number of defects and the severity of each defect may differ, owners invariably list some of the following defects as the most troublesome:

1. Automatic Hondamatic Transmissions 1974-1976. Shifting from forward to reverse, or drive to reverse, or drive to park, causes grinding. Possible sticky selector valve and weak selector valve spring. Any shifting no matter how slight, while car is in opposite motion, could damage gear box of transmission. Cannot rock in snow. Often damaged by transport loading and unloading.
Other transmissions. Standard blocking ring and ring syncro block is prone to failure due to improper assembly at the factory, usually within first 12,000 miles.

2. Differential. If you spin wheel in snow or sand, spider gear shaft may fail. Most other make cars can take this but not Honda. Breakdown easily blamed on owner.

3. Motor. Linebore may not be even on all models. Difficult to machine due to poor availability of over-sized bearings. Crankshaft journals (machined part of crankshaft) may also be unevenly machined. Connecting rods may be of uneven size and weight. All this makes engine rebuilding possible only with Honda parts and detailed instructions from Honda. Engine rebuilding very difficult.

Motor head gasket. 1976-1978 CVCC, Accord, and Civics motor head gaskets can destroy engine. There is no limit to warranty. Cam shaft oil seal on all models, all years, blows out due to high pressure in crankcase. Once warranty expires, Honda may refuse to pay for repairs. Oil pressure relief valve, for all models, may stick causing high oil pressure, blown gaskets, seals, and oil filters.

Crankshafts. Often damaged on 3rd and 4th cylinders. May be due to placement of preheat shield or radiator that leads to poor air circulation causing overheating.

Camshafts. On 1974-1978 all models, any mileage, cam lobes may wear down, causing illegal emissions and excessive fuel consumption.

Oil pump gear. On camshaft, may strip prematurely causing loss of oil pressure and engine destruction. The 3rd and 4th cylinders may go first.

Rocker arms. May wear early causing poor compression and possibly destroying camshaft.

Valve spring failures. On 1974-1975 models spring failure causes burnt exhaust valves up to engine no. EB 21076644.

Oil filter. On all models, both Honda and independent filters can loosen causing oil filter seal (gasket) to blow out. As a result, the engine self-destructs. If this occurs within the warranty period and with a Honda filter, Honda will repair for free. This also affects emission/pollution standards by dropping oil onto road.

Exhaust gasket pipe connecting manifold to exhaust pipe. On all Accords including prototypes and 1977-1978 station wagons vibrations may cause bolts to work loose, gaskets to burn out, and extremely hot and noxious exhaust fumes to enter engine and passenger compartments possibly causing serious safety hazard. This hot exhaust may also cause melting of carburetor-base gasket and heat insulators.

Pre-heater hose. Connecting exhaust to air cleaner, this may be located too close to fuel pump and could cause fuel perculation in fuel pump, giving poor engine performance and potential fire hazard if fuel pump sweats or leaks gasoline.

4. Brakes. All brakes (front) must be serviced every 5000 km/3000 m/3 mos. in normal weather and more frequently in winter. The cost for this is about $20. Calipers can seize on (engage) and won't return (disengage). If this occurs in winter with front wheel drive, it may cause loss of control of vehicle with one brake engaged, and one disengaged.

See Red Stamp Warning in owner's warranty book. Also poor or uneven adjustment of rear brakes may send car into a spin due to front-wheel drive. This poor adjustment may be caused by lack of proper pre-delivery inspection.

DANGER: Front passenger may activate brakes by pressing foot on firewall.

5. Rear wheel bearings. There is a possibility of premature failure on all 1974-1978 models.

6. Water pump pulley. Pulley may shear off on 1977-1978 Civics and Accords.

7. Water pump bearings. 1977-1978 Civics and Accords water pump may fail without warning.

8. Shock absorbers. On 1977-1978 station wagons and Accords shock absorbers are noisy, weak, and easily bent, which may affect front and rear wheel alignment and can be hazardous.

9. Wiper blades. 1977-1978 Accords' wiper blades are subject to streaking, smearing, freezing, and cracking.

10. Exhaust system. On station wagons and Accords are dangerous to drive with tailgate down because exhaust fumes are sucked into passenger compartment.

11. Batteries. Insufficient amperage prior to 1977 causing no starts, towing and boosting expenses.

12. Bumper fasteners. 1978 fasteners may be too weak to withstand shocks from minor impact.

13. Headlights. On all models for all years, due to high failure rate, Honda has secret 12/12 warranty. Low beam failures most common.

14. Door mirrors. On all 1978 models, mirrors work loose and may not keep adjustment.

15. Window regulators and channels. On all Civics, if a window is opened when frozen, regulator and channels may bend out of shape and occasionally damage door panel.

16. Poor cold air and noise insulation. Occurs in all years and models.

17. Bridgestone front tires. Station wagon tires may wear out as early as 8000 miles due to excessive tire vibration.

18. Heater control cable. Cable is too close to accelerator and may catch driver's right foot.

19. Seat fabric. On all CVCC models black and white checkered fabric may shed as early as first year.

20. Gas tank. Tank cap can be opened with any key or dime.

21. Poor gas mileage. Honda's motor defects and inadequate dealer servicing may actually reduce overall gasoline mileage.

Paint Defects and Premature Rusting
Of course, all cars have paint problems and very few are not vulnerable to premature rusting. And Honda is no exception. To the contrary, Honda owners complain that their cars are afflicted with paint and rust problems that are far from acceptable. Owners complaining about these problems are often told that the problems are normal and Honda cannot give rust or paint compensation after the normal 12-month warranty has expired.

While Honda dealers and zone representatives are telling owners that they must pay for all paint and rust problems themselves, Honda service officials are applying a secret warranty extension when dealing with owners who complain vigorously and won't take no for an answer. This schizophrenic approach to customer relations has resulted in a number of Honda owners doubting Honda's good faith.

All Honda models are covered by this secret warranty extension without second owner exclusion. Within 12,000 miles, or first year of service, Honda will pay full cost of stone chips paint damage. If rust or paint problems occur within 24 months or 24,000 miles, Honda Service Bulletin ASB66 provides for free paint or rust repairs. Up to 36 months or 36,000 miles Honda will provide free parts replacement of any perforated body panel.

When Honda first gave out its new car franchises, it was very careful to choose dealers who had proved their honesty and competency in dealing with customer problems. This policy helped the company to establish itself as being sincerely concerned with customer satisfaction. Nevertheless, as with the diminishing control of the quality of its new cars, Honda's dealer network, after 1977, began to lose sight of this goal and customer complaints concerning poor dealer servicing and unfair warranty administration increased at an alarming rate. Most of these service and warranty complaints fall into the following areas:

Warranty and Service Complaints
1. Unfair motor secret warranty extension
2. Unfair rust/paint secret warranty extension
3. Expensive repair work not requested
4. Incompetent repairs
5. Unnecessary repairs
6. Poor parts supply
7. Inadequate customer relations
8. Communication problems with dealer/company
9. High parts cost
10. Manufacturing defects dismissed with absurd rationalizations

A number of dissatisfied Honda customers stress that they would have been more tolerant with their car's flaws if the dealer network had shown as much skill in fixing defects as it had shown in selling new cars.

In addition to numerous parts defects, body problems, and poor warranty servicing at the dealership and company zone levels, many owners also report the existence of safety-related defects. These potentially dangerous defects fall into the following areas:

Potentially Hazardous Defects
1. Loss of steering
2. Wheel bearing failure
3. Chronic stalling
4. Brake failure
5. Passenger activating braking system
6. Sudden acceleration
7. Engine fires
8. Front axle cracking
9. Tire failures
10. Headlight failures

Usually when an automobile manufacturer is alerted to the presence of a potentially hazardous defect, steps are taken by the car maker to resolve the problem before government authorities and consumer protection groups becomed aware of the defect. However, in Honda's case, a number of owners have complained that their complaints were not acted upon despite the possibility that the problem could be safety-related.

Motor Failures and Head-Gasket Failures

The catastrophic breakdown of Honda motors can have consequences other than the inconvenience of being stopped with an immobile vehicle. A motor that can potentially deliver an unexpected explosion, fire, and mechanical parts debris can certainly create a lasting impression upon the most experienced driver.

Experts agree that Honda's head-gasket failures involve the corrosion of the steel head-gasket caused by a temperature differential in thermal expansion rates between the aluminum cylinder head and the cast-iron engine block.

It is estimated that the head-gasket failure repairs could cost from $400 to $800. Indications of head-gasket failure include white exhaust smoke at cold idle, poor gas mileage, excessive oil consumption, loss of oil pressure, engine stalling, and the odor of engine coolant present in the passenger compartment.

Because of the severity of Honda's motor and rust problems (presently under investigation by the Federal Trade Commission) the purchase of any used Honda represents a high risk venture at best. Toyota and Mazda would be better alternate choices.

Technical Specifications

Honda Civic:	1976	1977	1978	1979	1980
Wheelbase	86.6"	86.6"	86.6"	86.6"	88.6"
Length	146.9"	146"	146"	146"	148"
Width	59.2"	59"	59"	59"	62.2"
Weight	1632 lb.	1665 lb.	1674 lb.	1674 lb.	1790 lb.
Standard motor	4 cyl.	4 cyl.	4 cyl.	4 cyl.	4 cyl.
Gas mileage	31	32	34	33	31
Price	$1800	$2200	$2700	$3300	$3900

Not recommended

Honda Accord:	1977	1978	1979	1980
Wheelbase	93.7"	93.7"	93.7"	93.7"
Length	163"	163"	163"	163.2"
Width	64"	64"	64"	63.8"
Weight	1993 lb.	2022 lb.	2040 lb.	2187 lb.
Standard motor	4 cyl.	4 cyl.	4 cyl.	4 cyl.
Gas mileage	29	28	28	29
Price	$3500	$4200	$5100	$6000

Not recommended

Rusting Diagram for Honda Civic

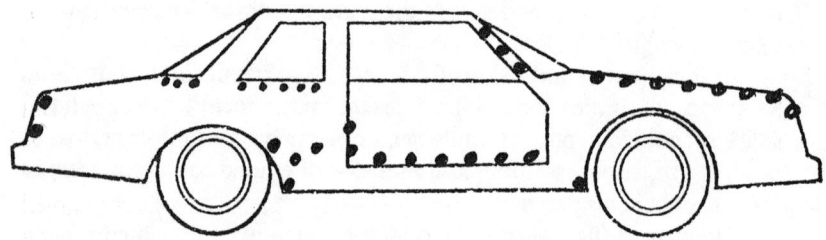

1976–1978

Defect Register

Affected Model   *Defect*
1975–1979 Honda Civic   Corrosive elements in the environment may cause deterioration of the front and rear lower suspension arms. This corrosion may result in loss of vehicle control.

1975–1977 Honda Civic 1200   Possibility that internal muffler pressure can create a split in the seam if the muffler is in deteriorated condition.

MAZDA

Mazda has come a long way from the time a few years ago when its name was synonymous with premature corrosion, motor failures, and mediocre servicing. In fact, since 1978, Mazda's vehicles have become so reliable and rust-resistant that their resale value has skyrocketed.

By offering its lowest-priced models for under $5000, Mazda competes favorably with other highly-rated subcompact cars like the Subaru, Colt/Arrow, Toyota.

But despite their attractively low selling price and reliable construction, Mazda vehicles are still poorly serviced by a weak dealer network that often turn minor repairs into major problems. Parts costs and availability leave a lot to be desired, and warranty support from Mazda is erratic at best.

Let us hope that these servicing and parts problems will be solved by Mazda's new North American management team. In the meantime, owners would be wise to shop around and use independent garages for more competent and less expensive servicing.

Mazda owners complain of defects affecting the motor (both conventional and rotary models), clutch, and braking performance. Mazda has extended the warranty to cover mechanical defects in the "O" rings of its rotary engines, which cause an excessive burning of oil due to improper internal sealing; however, many Mazda owners have complained that this warranty extension is not applied equitably to all rotary Mazda owners.

The 1972 and earlier Mazdas were particularly susceptible to failure of the rotor-housing water "O" rings, and accompanying overheating. First symptoms are usually hard starting, rough idling for 10 to 20 seconds after start, white exhaust smoke, and coolant loss. In the latter stages, overheating may occur. Should these symptoms occur, visit your local dealer to confirm the diagnosis. If confirmed, contact the Mazda Branch Service Representative for your area for information concerning Mazda's engine rebuilt/exchange program. All factory-rebuilt engines are equipped with an improved, Teflon-backed water "O" ring to reduce the chance of a second failure.

For Mazdas made before 1978, both the conventional and rotary-motor models are unacceptable used-car buys. Conventional models are similar to Datsun and Toyota cars except that warranty performance and dealer servicing are not as good. Parts are often unavailable and costly. The dealer network is very weak and the national Mazda office has recently undergone a complete reorganization. Depreciation is also rapid with these models. Owners report that the major problems with conventional Mazda models are defective motors, transmissions, and brakes.

Mazda rotary models, equipped with the "revolutionary" rotary engine, are much more expensive than their conventional counterparts. Depreciation, however, is just as rapid as Mazda's other models and repairs to the engine may be necessary every few months. The rotary engine has benefited from several warranty extensions, but Mazda rotary owners find that many dealers are ill-equipped to repair their engines properly. In California, Mazda has been charged by the state consumer protection authorities with not fully respecting the Mazda warranty extensions. Mazda now boasts that its new five-year/75,000 mile rotary warranty for all new models is the best warranty in North America. It is not likely that owners of early Mazda models would agree.

So although the post-1978 models are worth considering, if you're looking at older cars you'd do best to stay away from used Mazdas and check out Honda, Toyota, or Datsun first.

Technical Specifications

Mazda GLC:	1977	1978	1979	1980
Wheelbase	91"	91"	91"	91"
Length	168"	160"	168"	156"
Width	63"	63"	63"	63.2"
Weight	1965 lb.	1940 lb.	1900 lb.	1875 lb.
Standard motor	4 cyl.	4 cyl.	4 cyl.	4 cyl.
Gas mileage	29	28	29	29
Price	$1700	$2200	$2700	$3500

Recommended

Rusting Diagram for Mazda

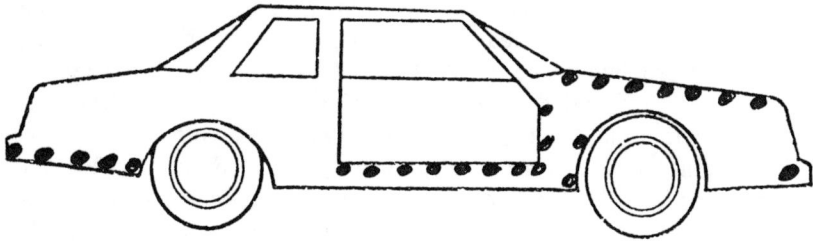

ALL MODELS (1974–1977)

Defect Register

Affected Model
1974 Mazda RX-4 sedan, hard top and wagon

Defect
Possibility that when engine is started, steering wheel will turn by itself, forcefully, in either direction due to improper tolerance within reaction sensing system. This could be caused by turning steering wheel without power steering pump in operation. (Correct by inspecting and replacing complete gearbox assembly.)

1974 Mazda pickup trucks

Possibility that exhaust pipe protector may be deformed, resulting from hitting projection on ground in vehicle off-road use. Should protector be crushed into exhaust pipe, shield surface temperature could rise to point where dry grass could smolder. This could occur only if vehicle is parked in tall dry grass and grass is in contact with protector. (Correct by installing additional protector underneath existing protector.)

1981 Mazda GLC vehicles equipped with air conditioners

Deterioration of the catalyst may occur due to the unintentional operation of the throttle positioner system which can affect the level of exhaust emissions.

SUBARU

Considered by many motorists as the Japanese counterpart to the Volkswagen Beetle, Subaru has greatly improved since its early egg-shaped problem-prone pre-1972 models. Its early models were automotive freaks, with doors that opened into the wind and quality-control defects that may have given Consumers Union nightmares.

Since those early experimental days, though, Subaru has become a new-car buy that is incomparable in overall driving performance and fuel economy. With front-wheel drive and a low sticker price, the Subaru rivals only the top-rated Toyota in engineering excellence. Servicing, parts supply, and a rapid depreciation rate combine to place the Subaru first in the Japanese lineup of recommended new- and used-car buys.

Since 1973 Subaru has worked hard to create an image of an automobile manufacturer that makes inexpensive and reliable vehicles, styled for maximum efficiency.

This philosophy of innovative design and economical performance has permitted Subaru to increase its dealer network in the United States to more than 700 dealers and increase its retail sales considerably.

Subaru's 1980–1981 models are longer, lower, and wider than their predecessors, but their curb weight is slightly increased. This increase in weight has had no effect upon gas economy which varies between 28–30 MPG for the sedan, and 26 MPG with the Brat.

Gas economy is achieved without a catalytic converter (except for manual transmission sedan and hardtop versions); however, all of the post-1979 vehicles require unleaded fuel.

Although parts supplies may be a problem in some rural areas and in the West, parts cost and durability are more than reasonable.

Dealer servicing has remained relatively complaint-free except for some discontent voiced by Subaru owners upset over inadequate servicing of the front-brake calipers.

Warranty performance is another plus for Subaru. Because the car is so well assembled and relatively defect-free, the manufacturer's warranty performance is less critical than it is with other car makes. Still, owners of 1974–1980 models report warranty repairs are usually carried out efficiently, promptly, and without recriminations.

One area of particular concern is Subaru's pricing policies. By pricing its vehicles more than $1000 less than comparative, competitive models, Subaru guarantees its dealers a steady stream of buyers all anxious to sign purchase contracts. Unfortunately, some Subaru dealers are jacking up the low manufacturer's suggested retail price with inflated transportation and prep charges that can drive the price up hundreds of dollars.

Rusting Diagram for Subaru

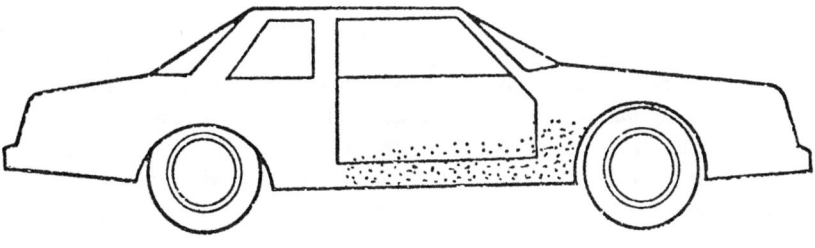

ALL MODELS (1973-1974)

Technical Specifications

Subaru:	1977	1978	1979	1980
Wheelbase	96.9"	96.9"	96.9"	93.7"
Length	163"	164"	164"	164.2"
Width	60"	61"	61"	61"
Weight	1950 lb.	1975 lb.	2000 lb.	2020 lb.
Standard motor	4 cyl.	4 cyl.	4 cyl.	4 cyl.
Gas mileage	30	31	30	29
Price	$1400	$1800	$2200	$3000

Recommended

Defect Register

Affected Model
1976-1977 Subaru station wagons

Defect
An assembly jig modification resulted in an increase of clearance between the latch and striker of the back-door lock so that there is insufficient engagement of the latch and striker to prevent the back door from opening while the vehicle is in motion.

Affected Model
1980 Subaru GL model vehicles

Defect
Certain front seat belt assemblies manufactured by NSK Warner Ltd. (models NSB 1020-1022) may become unlatched under high belt loads such as those experienced in a collision.

TOYOTA

The Toyota Corolla is one of the best Japanese cars on the market. The dealership network is strong, servicing is not costly, parts are inexpensive and easily available, and depreciation is about average.

The best pre-1975 Toyota models were the 1971–1973 Corolla 1600 and 1200 models. These cars were spacious, rugged, and easy to service. Three major problems with the Corolla were the defective motor on the 1971 and 1972 model years, malfunctioning carburetors with the 1974–1975 models, and severe rusting of the front fenders (again, like Datsun) from 1970–1973. Toyota extended the warranty to cover the motor, carburetor and rusting defects, but second owners have not been formally included into the deal. Corona models cost more, but seem to offer no additional advantages than what one can get with the Corolla models.

Mechanical defects reported most frequently by Toyota owners over the last five years were problems with the motor, carburetor, brakes, air conditioner, and chassis construction.

In 1980 Toyota introduced a restyled Corolla. This car is an excellent used-car buy due to its peppier motor, improved brake components, and increased rust-resistance. The 1981 models should prove to be even better used-car investments, with a lower frequency-of-repair rate.

The front-wheel-drive Toyota Tercel is one of the most reliable and least expensive subcompacts on the market. Offered in two-door sedan and two-door hatchback body styles, the Tercel uses a 1.5-liter (88.6 cubic inches) in-line four-cylinder motor that is mounted longitudinally instead of transversely. The Tercel also has other standard features — such as rack-and-pinion steering, independent MacPherson strut suspension, and radial tires — that improve performance without increasing the car's retail price.

Technical Specifications

Toyota Corolla/Tercel:	1976	1977	1978	1979	1980
Wheelbase	93.3"	93.3"	93.3"	94.5"	98.4"

Toyota Corolla/Tercel:	1976	1977	1978	1979	1980
Length	164.6"	164.6"	165"	166"	160"
Width	61.8"	61.8"	61.8"	63"	61"
Weight	2266 lb.	2225 lb.	2235 lb.	2190 lb.	1874 lb.
Standard motor	4 cyl.	4 cyl.	4 cyl.	4 cyl.	4 cyl.
Gas mileage	27	26	27	28	35
Price	$1800	$2400	$3300	$4000	$4900

Recommended

Toyota Celica:	1976	1977	1978	1979	1980
Wheelbase	98.2"	98.2"	98.5"	98.5"	98.4"
Length	174"	174"	174.6"	175"	175.5"
Width	63"	63"	63.8"	64"	64.6"
Weight	2490 lb.	2490 lb.	2530 lb.	2470 lb.	2600 lb.
Standard motor	4 cyl.	4 cyl.	4 cyl.	4 cyl.	4 cyl.
Gas mileage	26	26	26	26	27
Price	$3100	$3700	$4300	$5400	$6400

Recommended

Rusting Diagram for Toyota

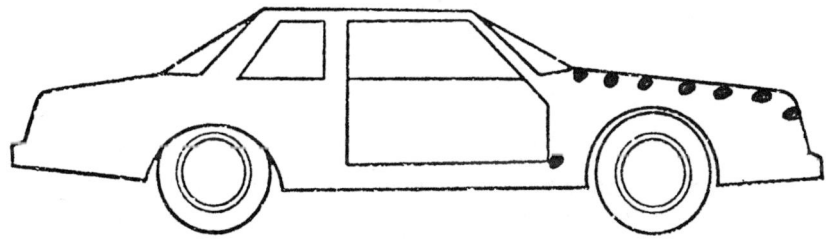

ALL MODELS (1974–1977)

Defect Register

Affected Model	*Defect*
Mark II (Produced for U.S.A. June, 1969, to June, 1970)	Possibility that during cold weather brake fluid may not adequately flow between reservoir tank and master cylinder. This condition would permit gradual accumulation of air into master cylinder system, resulting in soft pedal during application of brakes. (Correct by installing improved master cylinder components.)
1965-1970 Corona, 1970-1971 Corolla	Possibility that items placed in package tray under the right dash panel may inadvertently fall over protective partition and cause possible malfunction of accelerator linkage. (Correct by installing new partition.)
1971 Corolla 1200 sedan, coupe, station wagon 1971 Corolla 1600 sedan, coupe, station wagon	Possibility that engine stall or engine hesitation may occur due to malfunctions in evaporative emission control system. Engine hesitation or stall may be hazardous in road driving due to lack of fuel or loss of power after prolonged high-speed driving. (Correct by inspecting and modifying emission control system.)
1980 Toyota Celica and Corona vehicles and Corolla trucks	Vehicles equipped with 20R engines may have an engine vacuum pipe which can crack resulting in increased exhaust emissions. Possibility that during process of assembling component, lock nut was mistakenly not torqued on steering gear box worm gear bearing adjustor.

SAAB

Since 1961, Saab has been selling its Swedish economy car in North America as a direct competitor to the highly publicized Volvo. Despite its early start, however, Saab has never been recognized by the motoring public as a credible alternative to the Volvo. In fact, some motoring magazines have characterized the early Saab owners as "intellectuals" and "misfits."

Actually, Saab is a much better car than the Volvo, especially in view of the rapid decline in Volvo quality since 1972. Gas mileage is excellent, and driving performance is everything one would expect in a European car. As with the Volvo, Saab has a rapid depreciation rate, but due to Saab's lower initial cost, the total financial loss is minimized.

Servicing is one major deficiency reported by Saab owners. Because of its small franchised dealer network, Saab of Sweden and its American importers have been criticized by Saab owners for concentrating on the sale of new vehicles while used-vehicle servicing is neglected. The Washington-based Center for Auto Safety has been petitioned by one group of irate Saab owners for help in resolving what the owners' group collectively calls their "Saab story."

Saab has many of the same quality-control defects with its malfunctioning carburetor and electrical system as the Volvo. Owners report, though, that the manufacturer is very liberal in applying the warranty, even if the mileage or period of ownership warranty limitations have been exceeded.

Technical Specifications

Saab 99:	1976	1977	1978	1979	1980
Wheelbase	97.4"	97.4"	97.4"	97.4"	97.4"
Length	174"	174"	175"	175"	175"
Width	66.5"	66.5"	66.5"	66.5"	66.5"
Weight	2560 lb.	2670 lb.	2670 lb.	2486 lb.	2640 lb.
Standard motor	4 cyl.	4 cyl.	4 cyl.	4 cyl.	4 cyl.
Gas mileage	24	22	21	21	21
Price	$4000	$4700	$5400	$6500	$8900
Recommended					

Rusting Diagram for Saab

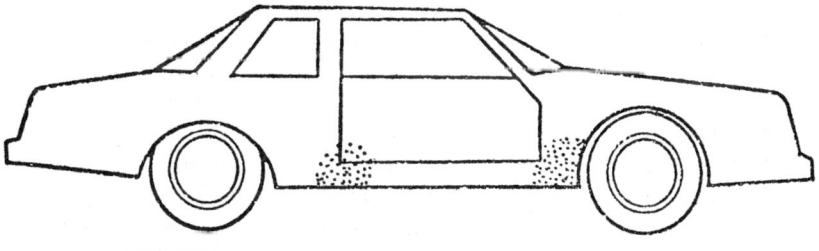

ALL MODELS (1974–1976)

Defect Register

Affected Model	*Defect*
1976 Saab 99 EMS, GL Wagonback and two-door vehicles	The door-sill plates have been improperly installed and may catch and pinch the front seat belts. This may result in cut or torn seat belts.
All 1975 Saab 99 vehicles and all 1976 Saab 99 vehicles up to serial number 99762039231 or 99767007278	Possibility of an improper installation of the original brake drawrod pivot pin. Should either of the pivot pins disengage from the drawrod, there would be a complete loss of service brakes.
All 1975 and 1976 model 99 Saab vehicles built through February, 1976	Ice formation in the throttle valve housing may form when outside temperature is below 20°F.
1976 and 1977 Saab-Scania 99	Possibility that fuel return line to tank was installed so that rear axle could contact line when suspension bottoms.
1980 Saab 99, 900	Possibility that on certain vehicles the mounting collar for the electric fuel pump, which is submerged in the fuel tank, could partially detach from the top of tank and cause a potential for fuel leakage.

VOLVO

By directing much of its advertising to what it calls the "leisure class" and arrogantly boasting of its engineering refinements, Volvo provides potential customers with a preview of its attitude, which has turned many Volvo owners sour on the car.

Owners complain of repeated mechanical failures involving the carburetor (hard starting and excessive fuel consumption), electrical system (tune-ups are often a monthly affair), and a fuel-injection system by Bosch that leaks gasoline to such an extent that the National Highway Traffic Safety Administration has ordered that the problem be investigated to determine if a safety-related defect exists.

Up until 1973, Volvo had one of the best reputations in America for providing its customers with well-built cars and for providing a strong warranty to cover what small defects might have cropped up. But time marches on, and Volvo's customer-relations policies and reputation have since changed dramatically. Owners complain that Volvo's warranty is no longer as liberal in practice as it once was, and what free warranty service is provided is handed out like food stamps to the needy.

Because of quality-control problems, Volvo has extended the guarantee on the fuel-injection assembly and carburetor for 36,000 miles without restriction to first owners.

For the past several years, the Automobile Protection Association has received a steady stream of complaints from Volvo owners.

Documented complaints from disenchanted and irate Volvo owners confirm that the expectations created by Volvo's clever advertising campaigns have not been fulfilled by either the car or dealer service. In fact, it appears to be obvious that Volvo had serious problems with persistent mechanical defects throughout the 1974–1976 model years and dealers who fail to diagnose and repair these defects properly.

Angry Volvo owners report frequent mechanical defects affect all major components of their cars. Subsequent repairs at their dealers are said to be costly, inadequate, and often only temporary.

Although not all Volvos have the same number of defects and the severity of each defect may differ, owners writing to the APA invariably list some of the following defects as the most troublesome:

Defective Parts

1. Fuel injection system
2. Gas tank assembly and filler
3. Transmission breakdown
4. Premature rusting
5. Paint peeling
6. Muffler and exhaust system
7. Brakes
8. Shock absorbers
9. Heater fan motor
10. Heater control
11. Heater thermostat
12. Air conditioner
13. Motor
14. Camshaft
15. Spark plugs
16. Transmission clutch
17. Starter
18. Leaky trunk
19. Leaky windshield
20. Rapid tire wear
21. Windows
22. Windshield wipers and washers
23. Radio
24. Locks
25. Oil warning light
26. Fuel pump
27. Fuel filter
28. Battery
29. Seats
30. Regulator
31. Alternator
32. Carburetor
33. Gas gauge
34. Clutch
35. Fan clutch

36. Fuses
37. Wheel bearings
38. Handbrake
39. Turn indicators
40. Clock

In addition to the already mentioned defective parts, Volvo owners also complain that their cars have bizarre and abnormal performance characteristics that are unacceptable. Although quite a few of the problems associated with Volvo performance can be explained as being due to mechanical defects and inadequate corrective repairs by dealers, some of the frequently reported problems are most probably caused by dealers who do not adequately inspect their cars before delivery. Nevertheless, regardless of the cause, Volvo owners report that their cars behave so erratically that they appear to be "possessed."

Performance Problems
1. Difficult starting
2. Excessive oil burning
3. Excessive gas consumption
4. Electrical system failures
5. Lack of power
6. High maintenance costs
7. Motor overheating
8. Oil leaks
9. Poor suspension
10. Unreliable
11. Poor quality control
12. Poor ignition
13. Engine knocking
14. Frequent breakdowns
15. Unreliable steering

It is interesting to note that one common complaint voiced by many Volvo owners concerned starting the car. This problem is further aggravated by the number of people who have trouble with *hot* weather starts. It is obvious that Volvo recognizes this problem since many owners can now purchase a "Hot Start Kit" to rectify these problems. It has not been confirmed whether Volvo has developed a "Cold Start Kit" yet, but one would certainly hope so.

Obviously, it is patently absurd for Volvo to have manufactured a starting system inappropriate for the climate of the country to which it is being exported in large numbers. Few owners appear to be aware of the starting kit's existence. It is evident that Volvo has an obligation to inform its customers of the kit's availability and that it offers to install the kit, without charge, to owners who request it.

Gas and oil mileage is also the subject of frequent complaints by Volvo owners. The number of persons reporting low gas mileage, fuel leakage, and seemingly chronic oil burning appears to be at odds with

Volvo's claim of gas-mileage economy. In some cases, this problem may be directly attributable to air-conditioning units, which can cut gas mileage significantly. Nevertheless, this certainly does not apply in all cases, and Volvo's customer relations personnel should no longer disclaim responsibility by claiming that excessive oil and gas consumption is "normal." The answer must lie in Volvo's engineering, and a review of recent improvements in such areas as exhaust-system design and electronic fuel injection would seem mandatory if Volvo really wishes to avoid a reputation for shoddy workmanship.

The list of other complaints and defects is lengthy. Such poorly engineered components as exhaust systems and mufflers that corrode easily, air-conditioning units that leak and reduce engine performance, leaking fuel injectors, and poorly designed heater assemblies are all recurring themes in APA addressed letters and phone transcripts. These tales of woe are all the more troublesome in light of Volvo's advertising campaign which promises economy and trouble-free driving. One can only wish that Volvo's engineers were as competent as its ad men.

The purpose in analyzing the APA's complaints concerning Volvo is threefold. It seems that owners' complaints may not be getting to the right people at Volvo. From reading the complaint letters, one gains the impression that Volvo's customer relations effort are Neanderthal at best. Is it really necessary for customers to sue Volvo, as three customers already have done, in order to get treated decently? Is it appropriate for Volvo to threaten to sue the TV program "Marketplace" in response to unfavorable criticism? Or, does it really help Volvo's image to sue a dissatisfied customer who tells his tale of mechanical frustration on television? This knee-jerk reaction to constructive criticism must be checked.

The second purpose of this report is to document the need for steps to be taken to review and analyze current Volvo quality-control standards. Programs must be initiated to insure that this spate of unconscionable mechanical breakdowns ceases immediately. Surely an automobile manufacturer who has attained Volvo's level of technological competence should be able to easily identify, correct, and, in the future, avoid problems which are annoying at best and lethal at worst. Obviously, the degree of defects that may be hazardous must take priority. Some of those defects reported by owners are:

Potentially Hazardous Defects
 1. Gas-tank leaks from flange of the drainage plug

2. Gas-tank leaks from crack in the neck of the feed-in tube
3. Gas-tank leaks from crack in crease
4. Windshield washers and wipers failing
5. Inadequate defrosting
6. Faulty steering
7. Inadequate locks
8. Exhaust system causing trunk and passenger floor to overheat
9. Steering wheel separation
10. Water leaking into side marker lights
11. Turn signal failures
12. Exhaust fumes in passenger compartment
13. Gasoline smell in passenger compartment
14. Windshield falling out
15. Emergency brake failure
16. Sudden steering loss
17. Imploded gas tank
18. Seatbelt warning light failure
19. Driver seat failure
20. Exhaust rubbing against car chassis
21. Concealed transport damage
22. Poor illumination of instrument panel
23. Wheel rims overheating
24. Exploding heater
25. Sticking gas pedal

Despite the fact that Volvo claims its cars are the safest vehicles they can make, a perusal of some owner complaints does not seem to support the claim that Volvo cars are completely safe. In fact, government-conducted tests have recently demonstrated that 1980 Volvos crashed into a fixed barrier at 35 mph provide so little occupant protection that both the driver and passengers would not survive the crash. Yet, both the Chevrolet Chevette and Chrysler Omni passed the crash test without "losing" the driver or passengers in the test cars.

Finally, the analysis of consumer complaints directed against Volvo has shown that the expectations created by Volvo's national advertising campaign are monumentally misleading and deceptive when viewed against the often unpleasant realities of Volvo ownership. Specific contradictions include cost of ownership, reliability, and durability. Volvo should immediately take steps to insure that its advertising conforms to this reality reported by far too many owners to ignore. Actually, Volvo should just concentrate more on improving its product than on maintaining its slipping image.

Service Complaints
1. Costly nonmaintenance service
2. Incompetent repairs (would you believe a pair of pliers left in transmission?)
3. Lack of parts
4. Inadequate predelivery inspection
5. Refusal of warranty claim
6. Slow repairs
7. No courtesy car available
8. Rude personnel
9. Unauthorized repairs
10. Repairs not needed
11. Promises not kept
12. Incorrect owner-registration card
13. No response to complaints
14. Bankrupt dealer
15. Poor diagnostic procedures

Technical Specifications

Volvo 242:	1976	1977	1978	1979
Wheelbase	104"	104"	104"	104"
Length	192.6"	192"	192"	192"
Width	67.3"	67.1"	67"	67.1"
Weight	2925 lb.	2814 lb.	2800 lb.	2800 lb.
Standard motor	4 cyl.	4 cyl.	4 cyl.	4 cyl.
Gas mileage	28	25	26	25
Price	$3700	$4500	$6900	$7500

Not recommended

Volvo 264:	1976	1977	1978	1979
Wheelbase	104"	104"	104"	104"
Length	192"	192"	192"	192"
Width	67"	67"	67"	67"
Weight	3197 lb.	3157 lb.	3000 lb.	3100 lb.
Standard motor	6 cyl.	6 cyl.	6 cyl.	6 cyl.
Gas mileage	20	19	19	18
Price	$8100	$8700	$9000	$11,000

Not recommended

Rusting Diagram for Volvo

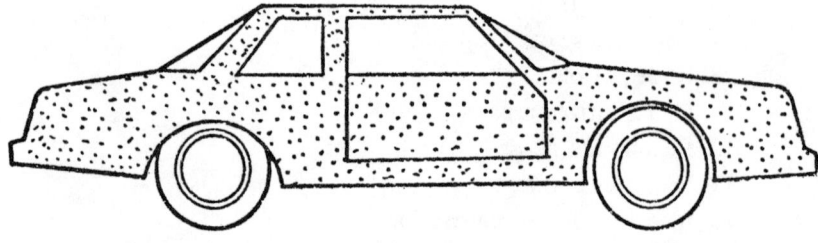

ALL SEDANS (1970–1973)

Defect Register

Affected Model

1975–1976 Volvo models equipped with standard steering.

MODEL	VIN RANGE
242	4330-74555
244	7905-119705
245	4680-75572

Defect

The four bolts securing the ball joint may loosen, resulting in a noticeable suspension noise which, if left uncorrected, may result in front-suspension collapse. Also the fasteners securing the steering rack assembly to the subframe may loosen and may lead to loss of steering control.

APPENDIX

SELLING A CAR WITHOUT FEAR AND LOATHING

Selling your used car privately can be a profitable venture if the basics of good salesmanship and an honest approach are used. The most important thing to remember is that there exists a large market for reliable used cars in the $1000–$2500 range and most people prefer buying from individuals than professional used-car salesmen. One of the major obstacles in selling a used car privately is convincing the buyer that the vehicle is not being sold because it is a "lemon." By using the following suggestions your used cars should be sold quite easily.

1. *Write an effective want ad.* See p. 190
2. *Don't sell to friends or family members.* Anything short of perfection, and you become the local leper.
3. *Don't touch the odometer.* You may get a few hundred dollars more for your car, but you also may get a criminal record.
4. *Paint the car.* Some specialty shops charge only $100 and give a guarantee.
5. *Make minor repairs.* This includes a minor tune-up and patching up exhaust.
6. *Clean the car.* Use a reconditioning firm or spend the weekend scrubbing the interior and exterior.
7. *Buy new or retread tires.* Retreads may cost $10–$15 each, are not less safe than regular tires, and are offered in radial style.
8. *Let the buyer examine the vehicle.* Insist vehicle be inspected by an independent garage. Be sure to accompany owner to garage.
9. *Keep important documents handy.* Show prospective buyers the sales contract, repair orders, owner's manual, and all other documents that show how car has been maintained and can authenticate the mileage.
10. *Don't mislead the buyer.* If the car was in an accident, or some financing is still to be paid, admit it. Any misleading statements may later be used in court against you. It is also advisable to have someone witness the actual transaction in case a future dispute arises.
11. *Know the car's value.* Study newspaper dealer ads and compare them with the used-car values listed in this guide. Undercut the dealer price by $200–$300 and be ready to bargain down another ten percent for

serious buyers. Remember, used-car prices can fluctuate wildly depending upon which car has become a fad, so watch the want ads carefully before pricing your used car.

Many of these suggestions may not be practical for some sellers of used cars in the $300–$1000 range. Nevertheless, no matter what price the used car is selling for, as long as there is no attempt by the seller to deceive or trick the buyer, everything should go smoothly.

HOW TO WRITE A GOOD WANT AD

1. *Start your advertisement with the name of the car you have to offer.* Give company, model, and year.
2. *Give information clearly, including price.* Readers react more quickly and favorably when given complete or definite information. One of the most important considerations in any advertisement is to include the price.
3. *Make it easy for the prospect to reach you.* Always include your telephone number or your name and address. If you do not have regular hours, state a preferred time to have prospects contact you.
4. *Use consecutive insertions for the greatest reader response.* A seven-day order is best and costs less per insertion. There are also special monthly rates for those who want to keep their name and offers before the public each and every day. You can stop the ad when you get the desired results.
5. *Place yourself in the reader's position.* Ask yourself what you would want to know if *you* were buying a used car. The answer you give will make a good classified ad.
6. *Remember that classified readers are already in the market to buy.* So give them every advantage you can with good ad copy. It could make the difference between response and nonresponse.

Want ads that fail usually do so not through lack of readership, but because they are carelessly worded and do not contain enough information to get prompt action. Even an interested reader might pass up an ad that, for example, did not include a telephone number where the seller could be reached.

If you follow the guidelines listed above, you are almost sure to get good results. Your finished ad should look something like this:

'78 Chevy Nova 2 dr. 1 owner, 35,000 miles, power steering & brakes, $2900, call 555-1272 eves.

Clarity and brevity combine to make this ad appealing. All the basic information is covered, including the price, and the prospective buyer knows how and when to contact the seller.

Remember, a good want ad is your best selling tool. And it's easy to write want ads that get results.